FORBIDDEN
HISTORY
SACRED
TEXTS

Hidden Scriptures, Lost Gospels, and the Secrets of the Bible They Don't Want You to Know.

Ben Wilder

Copyright © 2025 Ben Wilder History Publisher

Ebook ISBN: 978-1-959581-82-6

Paperback ISBN: 978-1-959581-83-3

For More information you can reach us via info@historytaboo.com

Printed in the U.S.A

**FORBIDDEN
HISTORY**

Table of Contents

Introduction
The Bible They Don't Want You to Read

I magine holding a book that could change everything you thought you knew about God, history, and humanity itself—only to be told you weren't allowed to read it. For centuries, ordinary people were kept in the dark while powerful councils, kings, and priests decided which words were "sacred" and which would be banished to fire and oblivion.

The Bible you know today is only a fraction of the story. Hidden behind monastery walls, buried in desert caves, and locked inside the Vatican's impenetrable archives are **forbidden gospels, lost apocalypses, and secret prophecies** that paint a startlingly different picture of faith. These texts speak of angels who fell to earth and bred giants, of Jesus teaching hidden wisdom only to his closest disciples, of women elevated as apostles, and of shadowy rituals practiced in secret by early Christians.

But why were these writings silenced? Were they too dangerous—too threatening to the power of the church and empire? Or did they contain truths that could unravel the story carefully crafted by centuries of religious authority?

In 1945, a farmer in Nag Hammadi, Egypt, unearthed clay jars filled with gospels that no one had seen for nearly 1,600 years. Just two years later, shepherds near the Dead Sea stumbled across scrolls that challenged everything scholars thought they knew about Judaism and the world of Jesus. And in dusty monasteries, half-forgotten manuscripts like the Book of Enoch, the Gospel of Mary Magdalene, and the Apocalypse of Peter whisper secrets of a Christianity far stranger—and far richer—than the one passed down in pews and pulpits.

This book is not just about lost pages of scripture. It is about the battle for memory itself. **Who gets to decide what is "truth"? Who benefits when whole books of the Bible are erased? And what happens when those lost voices finally return?**

You are about to step into the shadows of history, into the vaults of suppressed scripture and forbidden words. Some of what you will read will shake your assumptions. Some of it may anger you. And some of it will leave you with more questions than answers.

That is the point.

Because once you know what was hidden, you can never look at the Bible—or the world—the same way again.

Part I — The Lost Books of the Bible

Chapter 1: The Forgotten Scriptures – How books vanished from the canon

A young copyist bends over a wooden desk in a dim room. Oil smoke stings his eyes, the fibers of papyrus scratch under his pen, and the margins crowd with notes from elders who expect him to choose wisely. He has space for only one more text before the quire is full. On his left lies a well-loved letter that the congregation reads aloud each week. On his right, a visionary book that thrills some, frightens others, and divides the house. He weighs which text will be copied, read, and remembered, and which will return to the shelf, then to dust. In that moment, a book either lives in the memory of the church, or it begins to vanish.

That small, practical moment, a scribe deciding what to copy, sits at the heart of how books outlived their rivals and how others slipped from view. Canon was not set in a single council with a single vote. It formed through thousands of local choices in houses and halls, in cities and deserts, across languages and empires. Politics mattered, yes, but so did parchment costs, travel routes, literacy, worship habits, and which stories believers found life-giving. This is the story of how some scriptures were forgotten, how others were pushed aside, and how a few, once lost, returned to us from caves and rubbish heaps with sand still clinging to their pages.

What a canon really is

A canon is a standard collection that a community reads as its rule of faith and practice. Think less of a royal decree, think more of a playlist that has gone gold in city after city until one day everyone assumes these are the songs you must know. Early Christian canons were reading lists that solidified slowly. Today, we inherit a New Testament of twenty-seven books, yet that tidy number hides a long history of debate. Some writings were once central in some places and unknown in others. Some hovered at the edges for centuries, then fell out of favor. Others were so beloved locally that they never felt the need to argue their case beyond their region.

Four filters repeatedly shaped those lists: connection to the apostles, agreement with the core rule of faith proclaimed in worship, wide usage across churches, and age close to the first generation. Those filters were not applied as a checklist in a boardroom. Communities lived them. A gospel read in Syria might travel slowly to North Africa. A letter defended in Rome might be suspect in Cappadocia. Over time, patterns converged, though not perfectly, and what we now call the canon came into focus.

Why books vanish

Books disappear for several reasons, and none of them acts alone. Fragile media decay; papyrus crumbles, and ink fades. Geography isolates; a text born in one language may never be translated widely. Copying is expensive; scribes choose winners because the budget forces them to choose. Power polices boundaries; leaders guard doctrine and, in times of crisis, tighten the playlist. Taste shifts; a style or theme that resonated with one generation may fall flat with the next. When these forces align against a book, it becomes rare, then unread, then unknown.

Other forces revive the forgotten. Archaeology digs up library caches in the sands of Egypt. A farmer opens a jar and finds a codex. Scholars piece together fragments from the ancient city dump of Oxyrhynchus. With each discovery, poems, homilies, gospels, acts, and apocalypses that failed the old tests return to the conversation and challenge the neatness of the story we learned.

The making of the winners: a quick orientation

In the first two centuries, believers read a mix of Israel's scriptures, now called the Old Testament, and new writings that circulated by hand. Collections emerged unevenly. There was an early four Gospel set, a core group of Pauline letters, and a cluster of pastoral and catholic letters. Some books moved in and out of favor. Hebrews puzzled many because its author does not identify himself. Revelation terrified some, inspired others, and drew fire for its fierce imagery. James, Jude, and 2 Peter lingered at the edges for a long time in some regions. But as bishops, teachers, and communities traded letters and lists, the center of gravity grew. By the fourth century, a recognizable shape had formed, then calcified.

Now, if those are the winners, who are the missing runners-up, and why did they fall away?

Case study: a shepherd who almost made it

There was once a book that many churches read as scripture, a text of visions and commandments focused on repentance and moral reform. It taught a stern, hopeful path for believers caught in sin, guided by an angelic figure who appeared as a shepherd. Leaders in Rome admired it. Some early lists placed it right after the prophetic books. Over time, however, doubts rose. The date felt late to many, after the apostolic age. It read more like a powerful sermon than a record of Jesus and his first witnesses. It stayed beloved as edifying reading, even called useful for instruction, yet it did not remain in the final twenty-seven. This is how close calls happen: a book is honored at the front of the sanctuary, then shelved just outside the line.

Reading *The Shepherd* in a Second-Century Roman House Gathering

Case study: a letter from Clement that slipped away

Another near miss looks exactly like what you would expect in the New Testament. It is a letter to the Corinthians, written from Rome, urging unity, humility, and order. It quotes Israel's scriptures, rehearses the story of Jesus, and reasons with calm authority. For a time, churches read it in the same gatherings where they read Paul, and some copied it in the same bound volumes as Paul's letters. So why is it not in your Bible? The author was not an apostle and wrote a generation later. The letter is priceless for history and doctrine, yet the filter of apostolic origin eventually ruled it out of the fixed set. Over time, it moved from scripture to classic, from pulpit to library.

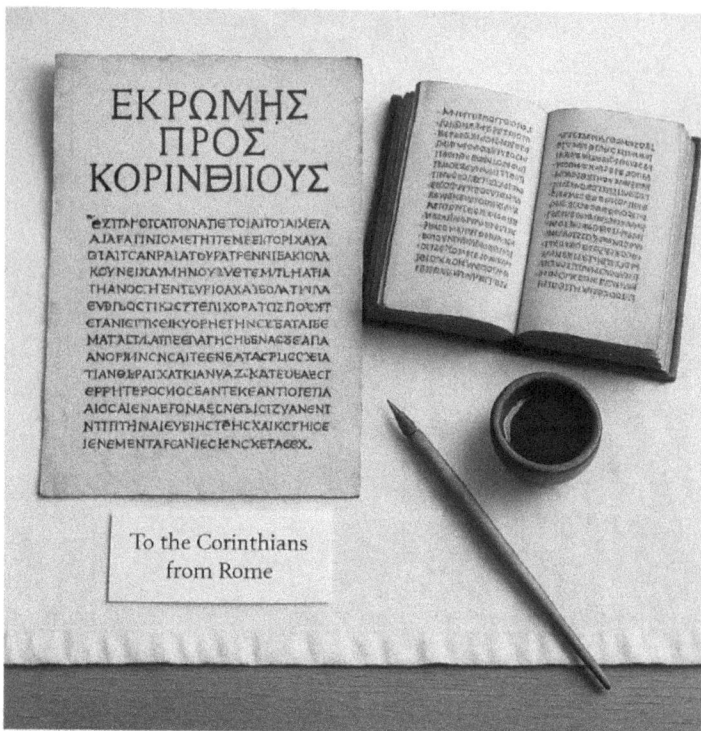

ΕΚΡΩΜΗΣ
ΠΡΟΣ
ΚΟΡΙΝΘΙΙΟΥΣ

To the Corinthians
from Rome

What to notice
The rare category called "ecclesiastical books" grew around the canon. Believers treated these writings with respect, read them aloud, and took counsel from them, but did not treat them as binding in every church. This category helps explain how cherished works could fade without scandal.

Case study: the infancy stories that charmed and troubled

New parents ask new questions, and the earliest gospels do not linger over the childhood years of Jesus. Later writers filled that gap with stories about his birth and youth. One text tells the tale of Mary's own parents and childhood, her betrothal, and Joseph's role as guardian. Another collection recounts boyhood episodes that range from mischievous to miraculous, as the young Jesus learns to master his power and his temper. These stories spread fast, shaped medieval imagination, and influenced art. Yet they entered the scene late, leaned on legends, and at times sent theological signals that the center did not trust. Their popularity could not overcome the age and authorship filter.

Case study: a visionary apocalypse that failed the final vote

Apocalyptic literature was a beloved genre in Jewish and early Christian circles. One early Christian apocalypse, circulating under an apostolic name, offered a vivid tour of the afterlife, including scenes of judgment that were quoted widely in the early centuries. For a time, some churches treated it as scripture, while others only as edifying. Critics worried that its graphic depictions could be misused. Questions about its authorship and date grew. In some regions, it lingered at the edge of the list; in others, it was read privately. Eventually, it left the fixed set and became a powerful conversation partner rather than the rule itself.

Apocalypse of Peter: Heavenly Throne and Judgment

The gospels that did not make the four

Four gospels rose to prominence and stayed there. Others circulated in smaller circles. Some collected sayings of Jesus without a narrative frame. Others presented dialogues with the risen Christ. A few took bold positions on theology, stressing secret teachings for mature disciples. Several contained penetrating wisdom, and some include sayings that echo well with the earliest traditions. Why did they vanish from the canon?

Three reasons dominate. First, authorship claims were often pseudonymous, a common practice in the era but one that later leaders distrusted. Second, many appeared or reached popularity after the four gospels had become a liturgical standard, which made it hard to displace the established set. Third, several took stances on creation, body, and salvation that clashed with the rule of faith repeated week after week in baptisms and creeds. In short, late timing, thin ties to apostles, and theological friction pushed them to the margins. That does not mean they lack value. It means they lost a complex contest where practice and doctrine met.

How leaders sorted writings without a single tribunal

The idea that one council at one time created the canon is tidy and wrong. Leaders wrote letters listing books they recommended and those they warned against. Teachers categorized texts as widely accepted, disputed, or rejected. Regional gatherings confirmed the books already read in their churches. No emperor imposed a list at the stroke of a pen. Instead, dozens of converging decisions hardened the center over time.

When persecutions struck, officials sometimes demanded that believers hand over their scriptures. Communities with limited resources had to decide which books to guard with their lives. That crisis forced clarity. After peace returned, the empire sponsored large Bible codices for major churches. Those projects are locked in choices by investing resources in expensive bound volumes. Once a cathedral had a beautifully made Bible, it was not likely to add new books lightly.

Scriptorium of Roman North Africa, c. AD 360
– Making a Giant Biblical Codex

The role of heresy hunters, and the value they preserved

Polemicists sometimes sound harsh, yet we owe them thanks for preserving quotations and summaries of books that no longer survive. When leaders argued that a community had strayed, they would quote the offending lines. Ironically, that preserved those lines when the original copy perished. In a few cases, the only reason we know a so-called lost book existed is because a critic listed it and objected to it.

This does not mean the critics invented their targets. It means debates leave traces. If a gospel taught secret knowledge to the few, leaders who championed public teaching for all would push back. If a treatise denied the goodness of creation, preachers grounded in Israel's scriptures would defend the body as God's good work. The clash sharpened boundaries and, by accident, preserved data that modern readers can now reassess with cooler heads.

Language and location, the great silencers

Books live when readers live near them. A text born in Syriac that never traveled into Greek or Latin had a steep hill to climb. A work beloved in Egypt might never find a patron in Rome. When a language's literary center collapses, the works written in that language suffer. Political shifts, trade routes, and communal migrations all influence what gets copied.

Translation is costly. A translator needs skill, time, and community buy-in. When a church has a tight reading list that fits its worship cycle, there is little incentive to fund a translation of something new. Many texts that we call lost did not vanish by decree; they died quietly because no one paid to copy them into the next language.

BOOK ROUTES AND LANGUAGE REGIONS OF TH EASTERN MEDITERRANEAN (c. 1st–4th centuries CE)

Asia Minor

Italy

ROME

JERUSALM

Seath

AXANCIA

GREEK
ARAMAIC
LATIN

JERUSALEM

ARAMAIC

EGYPT

LANGUAGE REGIONS
------- GREEK
———— ARAMAIC
———— LATIN

ALEXANDRIA

*Benzhmarked to standard historical atlases; routes after Roman mariiune trade maps.

Money, materials, and the economics of survival

Every page costs. Papyrus costs. Parchment costs more. Ink costs. A skilled scribe is paid, fed, and housed. A binding team must stitch quires and craft covers. Communities count coins and choose. If a codex can hold four gospels, that is efficient, so the four thrive. If a shelf can hold a few great volumes, long works have an advantage over many small scrolls. When codices rose to dominance over scrolls, multi-book collections became practical. That shift favored the fourfold gospel, the collected Paul, and the fixed set of catholic letters. Smaller, isolated writings struggled to find a place in those bound formats.

Politics, unity, and the fear of fracture

When a movement faces internal division, leaders simplify. They preach core summaries of the faith, baptize in a shared confession, and teach with short lists that everyone knows. This is not cynicism, this is crisis management. In the second and third centuries, intense debates about the nature of Christ, the value of the body, and the continuity with Israel's scriptures shook congregations. Leaders responded with a common rule of faith and with lists that embodied it. Writings that blurred those lines, even if treasured in pockets, lost ground.

Imperial favor did not create the canon, yet it amplified the impulse toward a stable center. When a church enters public life after persecution, it leans toward texts that unify worship across regions. That dynamic helped secure the final form and accelerated the forgetting of texts that had once mattered in smaller networks.

Council in a Fourth-Century Basilica: Books Read in the Liturgy

The Jewish canon question, and what it teaches

Many Christians tell a neat story that a Jewish council fixed the Hebrew canon in the first century. The real picture is more complex. Jewish communities also formed their collections over time, with local variation. Some texts were revered in some circles, contested in others. The point for our chapter is this: Christian communities emerged from a matrix where collections formed through usage, teaching, and copying, not through a single decree. That heritage shaped Christian habits. It explains why Christians could live with some books widely read and others debated for generations.

How a codex buried in sand changed the conversation

The sands of Egypt saved what economics and politics let drift away. In several sites, ancient Christians hid or stored codices that they did not keep for public reading. Heat and dryness turned those jars and caves into accidental archives. When modern diggers opened them, sayings collections and revelatory dialogues that had been missing for more than a millennium returned. Suddenly, readers could compare those words with the gospels they knew. Some sayings felt unfamiliar; others sounded like early friends. The rediscovered texts do not overturn the canon, but they show that the early Christian bookshelf was broader than the final list, and that the boundary between valued and rejected was complicated in real time.

The rumor and the reality of suppression

Did powerful leaders hide books to keep the truth from the people? It makes for a good thriller, yet the record is subtler. Leaders did argue strongly against books they believed endangered faith. They warned against doctrines that cut the story of Jesus away from the story of Israel or that demoted the value of bodies and the created order. They sometimes ordered texts burned during doctrinal crackdowns. These acts were real and severe. At the same time, sheer neglect and practical limits did more to erase books than any single purge. When copying slowed and translation stopped, a book's days were numbered, with or without a bonfire.

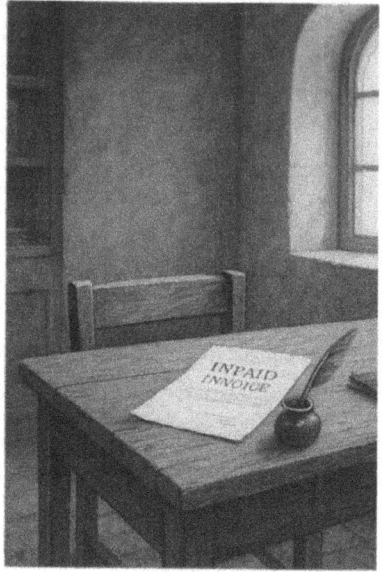

SUPPRESSION AND SILENCE
Civic Book Burning and an Unfunded Scriptorium

Neglect kills faster than fire

Burning a library is dramatic. Failing to fund a scribe is routine. Over centuries, the routine defeats the dramatic.

How to read a lost gospel without losing your balance

Approach a newly discovered gospel with curiosity and clarity. Ask: When and where was it written, and by whom? What audience needed this text at that time? How does it speak about creation, body, suffering, and love? Does it amplify the voice of Jesus that we already recognize from the earliest layers, or does it pull the story in a direction that the earliest worship did not take? Then, before drawing grand conclusions, read the four gospels again, listen to how they harmonize and argue, and place the new text alongside them. That is how to honor both the canonical center and the wider library that history nearly erased.

The quiet power of liturgy

Public reading shapes memory. If a book is read every week in worship, it weaves into the community's mind. If it is never read in worship, it rarely survives as more than a curiosity. Early Christian worship featured fixed readings from the law and the prophets, from the letters, and from the gospels. Over time, those cycles hardened. Books outside the cycles faded. The liturgical calendar thus acted as a conservator for some texts and as a gentle undertaker for others.

The copyist's hand and the bias of the margin

Scribes are human. They make choices, correct perceived errors, harmonize passages, and add clarifying notes. In a few cases, small glosses drifted into the main text in later copies of canonical works. In noncanonical works, marginalia sometimes reveal how readers were judging a passage. A scribe might write, "useful," "edifying," or "not to be read publicly." That one word can tell you why the work did not jump the fence into the fixed set.

When a lost work hides in plain sight

Sometimes a work survives because it was quoted so often that the quotations can be reassembled. Sometimes a later homily is really a digest of an earlier treatise. Sometimes a sermon cycle preserves a text long after its standalone copy was lost. Researchers piece threads together carefully, checking vocabulary, style, and theology. With enough threads, you can see the original pattern. This painstaking work brings back voices that would otherwise be silent.

Threads of Transmission

The haunting category of "we know this existed, but we do not have it."

Not every lost text will return. We have mentions of gospels, acts, letters, and apocalypses that no modern reader has seen. Some titles are tantalizing. A church father says someone wrote a gospel for a particular ethnic group, another mentions the acts of an apostle in a far region, and a letter is referenced that never appears in any codex we have. These missing works remind us that our picture, while rich, is partial. They warn us against overconfident theories. They also nudge us to value the accidental gifts that did survive.

INDEX OF LOST WORKS
(CLASSICAL ANTIQUITY)

Aristolte's On Comedy (?)

~~Aeschylus Achilleis~~

Sophocles *Tereus*

Euripides *Cresphontes*

~~Ovid Medea~~

Livy *Ab Urbe Condita*, Books XI–XX

~~Tacitus Annals, Books VII–~~ X

~~Cypria~~

~~Aethiopis~~

~~Nostoi~~

~~Iliou Persis~~

~~Telegony~~

Sappho Book 2 (?) = uncertain existence

status: lost

Index of Lost Works (Classical Antiquity)

Reading the margins without rewriting the center

There is a temptation to turn every rediscovered text into a revolution. Resist it. These works are precious, but treat them as voices in a crowded early room, not as secret keys that overturn everything. The core narrative, Jesus in the stream of Israel's story, crucified under a Roman ruler, raised, and confessed as Lord by communities across the empire, stands on early and broad testimony. The lost and found texts enrich, complicate, and sometimes correct our understanding of early diversity. They rarely uproot the center. Let them expand your sense of the early bookshelf and deepen your humility about the process, not rip out the foundation stones.

A human process guarded by a living community

Canon formation is a human process that took place in a living community under pressure, guided by prayer, preaching, and practice. If you seek a purely mechanical explanation, you will miss the heart. If you seek a purely conspiratorial explanation, you will miss the ordinary heroism of teachers, copyists, and patrons who kept books alive. The fact that our New Testament is both stable and well attested while including genres as different as a passion narrative, a missionary travel diary, and a dense apocalypse is itself a wonder. The fact that so many other works were loved for a season and then set aside is a sobering instruction in how communities conserve identity while surviving change.

Practical takeaways for a reader of forbidden history

First, expand your shelf. Add editions of the near misses and the lost and found. Read them beside the four gospels and the letters. Second, learn the timelines. Seeing which ideas appear when keeps you from romanticizing a late invention as an early secret. Third, learn how format, money, and language shape survival. Fourth, listen for the rule of faith, the melody that early churches sang, and compare how each text harmonizes or clashes. Fifth, keep a sense of proportion. The great story does not need protection from context, and the marginal texts do not need overstatement to be fascinating.

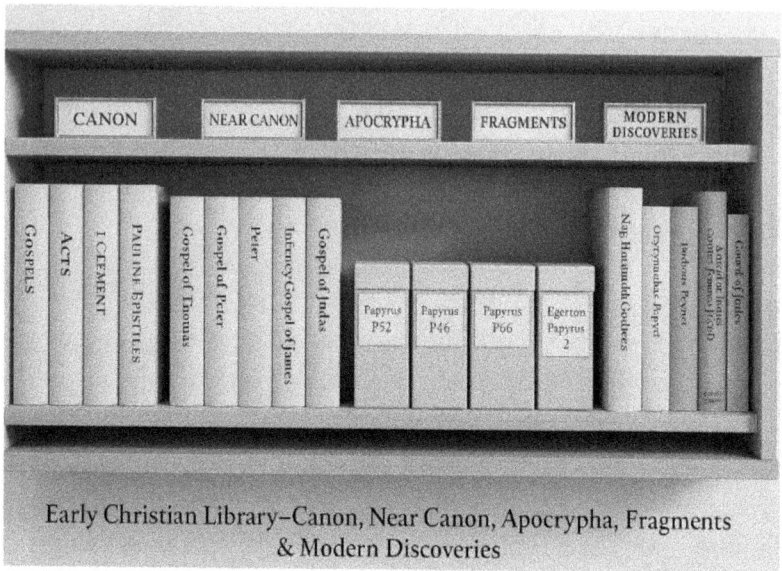

Early Christian Library–Canon, Near Canon, Apocrypha, Fragments
& Modern Discoveries

A brief tour of vanished or marginalized writings and their fates

A gospel that presents a resurrection scene where the cross itself speaks.
A set of acts where a fearless woman defies social expectations to preach
and suffer for her faith. A dialogue where the risen Jesus answers
questions about the soul's ascent. A wisdom collection of 114 sayings,
some familiar, some startling. An apocalypse that peers into the
mechanics of the heavens. Each reflects a real community's hope and
fear. Each found readers. Yet each hit a barrier, whether late
authorship, theological tension, or limited adoption.

Several of these works echo lines that feel ancient and true. Some carry
a mystical intensity that stirs the heart. Others bear marks of a later
taste, with long allegorical stretches or speculative cosmologies that
most churches eventually declined to canonize. Treat them the way a
historian treats a box of letters found in a grandparent's attic. Read
with attention. Hear the tone. Notice what was considered worth
writing and copying. Let the letters change how you see your family's
story, but do not forget the core events.

The danger of reading the past through our present disputes

Modern debates often recruit ancient texts as allies. That can be useful if done honestly. It can also distort. Early Christians argued about different things than we do. When we project our questions into their lines, we sometimes miss what they were actually trying to say. The safest course is to let each work speak in its own context, then ask careful questions about how it intersects with the center of the faith as lived and confessed by the broadest range of early communities.

The return to the beginning

Return to the scribe at his desk. His choice was not a conspiracy; it was a bet on what would feed his people. Sometimes he guessed right, sometimes he passed over a gem that no one in his time could afford to copy. We can honor his work by reading widely and wisely, by keeping both the playlist and the outtakes, by discerning the melody that carried the movement through fire and famine, and by enjoying the solos that did not make the final cut.

This is forbidden history in the only healthy sense, not a breathless hunt for scandal, but a patient recovery of the textures and choices that made our scriptures what they are and left many good books in the sand. If you listen closely, you will hear not one voice silencing many, but many voices, some loud, some quiet, moving toward a shared confession that took shape in the real world, under real costs, with real risks. The forgotten scriptures are not proof that someone hid the truth. They are proof that truth had to travel by foot, on sheets of papyrus, in crowded rooms, through risk and sacrifice. Some companions fell behind. We can pick them up now and learn from them.

If the phrase "forbidden history" stirs your curiosity, let it lead to better history, not to fantasy. Hold two truths at once. The canon we have was not inevitable; it was formed through choices, and some worthy books fell away. The canon we have is also remarkably strong, stable, and anchored close to the beginning. Reading the forgotten scriptures beside the received ones will not shrink your faith; it will enlarge your mind. It will also deepen your respect for the copyists, readers, teachers, and communities whose ordinary work carried extraordinary texts to us across two thousand years, while leaving footprints of many others in the sand.

At First Light: An Early Christian Coastal City (c. 3rd–4th century)

Chapter 2:

The Book of Enoch – Angels, giants, and forbidden prophecy

The story begins quietly, with a simple line from Genesis about a man who "walked with God." Then, without warning, the ground opens beneath the familiar Bible and we are plunged into a vast subterranean library: visions of crystalline palaces, star-gates that measure the seasons with relentless precision, shining beings who descend to teach forbidden arts, and the monstrous aftermath of their mistakes. This is the world of Enoch. When you read it closely, you stop asking why the book was lost and start wondering how it ever survived at all.

Meet Enoch, the man who would not die.

Enoch appears briefly in Genesis as seventh from Adam, a holy anomaly who "was not, for God took him." That sparsity is a literary wink. Second Temple Jews, eager to understand what it means to be taken alive by God, preserved a sprawling Enochic corpus that fills in the silence with audacity. Enoch, they say, was not merely righteous; he was chosen as a courtroom scribe for the cosmos, a messenger to rebel angels, a tour guide through the architecture of heaven. His archive, most famously 1 Enoch in Ge'ez, is not a single book; it is a library bound as one.

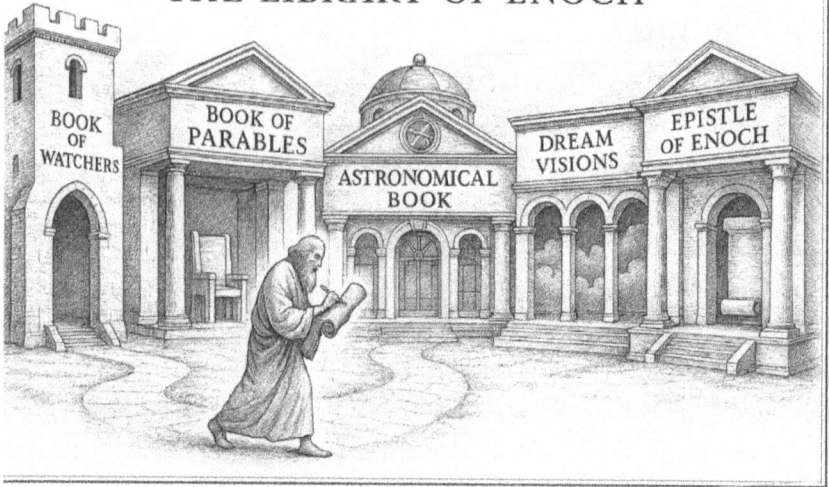

THE LIBRARY OF ENOCH

BOOK OF WATCHERS — BOOK OF PARABLES — ASTRONOMICAL BOOK — DREAM VISIONS — EPISTLE OF ENOCH

The five movements of 1 Enoch

1. Book of the Watchers, chs. 1–36: descent of angels, birth of giants, Enoch's visions and journeys.
2. Book of the Parables, chs. 37–71: the "Son of Man," judgment, and the Elect One.
3. Astronomical Book, chs. 72–82: a rigorous 364-day solar calendar and the laws of luminaries.
4. Book of Dream Visions, chs. 83–90: symbolic history of the world, including the Animal Apocalypse.
5. Epistle of Enoch, chs. 91–108: ethical exhortations, the Apocalypse of Weeks, and comfort for the righteous.

Why this material mattered to early readers

The Enochic archive answers questions that Genesis leaves deliberately underexplained. Where did violence come from so quickly after Eden? What are the "sons of God" in Genesis 6? Why does the world seem morally upside down? What does God plan to do about it? Enoch says: the rot began when powerful heavenly beings crossed a boundary, interfered with human culture, and hijacked knowledge itself. God's response, in this telling, includes both flood and future judgment. That is why Enoch's voice echoes in later Christian texts. Jude quotes Enoch directly about the Lord arriving with myriads to judge, and 2 Peter adapts the vision of sinning angels reserved for gloomy chains. Whether or not you accept Enoch's canonicity, you cannot miss its fingerprints on biblical imagination.

The Book of the Watchers: a scandal in the high places

At the heart of Enoch's drama is a mutiny. Two hundred angels, the "Watchers," descend on Mount Hermon, swear an oath, and take wives from the daughters of men. Their leaders, often named Shemihazah and Azazel, do not merely sin in private; they scale it. They teach metallurgy for weapons, cosmetics that eroticize, enchantments, root-cutting, and astrology for omens. In a stroke, the story reframes cultural power: technology, adornment, and arcane knowledge are not neutral in a broken world; they can be weaponized to magnify injustice.

The children of these unions, the giants, are insatiable. They devour human labor, then humans, then each other. Creation staggers under the weight of hybrid violence. The righteous cry out. Heaven hears.

Archangels respond. Michael, Gabriel, Raphael, and Uriel petition the Most High, who issues sentences. The Watchers are bound in deep places until the day of judgment. Azazel is singled out, chained in a stony desert until the end, because his teachings polluted everything. The giants die in the flood, yet their spirits linger as unclean forces that harass the living. Against this terror, Enoch is commissioned to speak. Imagine the scene: a human envoy delivering letters of doom to towering celestial criminals. Enoch does not flinch. He writes, he intercedes, he learns why mercy has limits when power preys on weakness.

Giants, facts and fables

Enoch's giants are symbols of multiplied harm and, in the story world, literal offspring. That combination has fueled centuries of speculation. Some readers chase evidence of titanic skeletons; internet hoaxes thrive; modern myths mushroom. Respect the text, then set down the fables. Enoch's point is moral clarity: when knowledge is divorced from wisdom and power crosses the boundary of creation, the result is predatory scale. The giants are the narrative body of that truth.

Giants and the temptation of spectacle

Enoch does not ask you to hunt bones. It asks you to take responsibility for the ways technology, glamour, and arcane leverage can turn human beings into commodities. The "giant" you can verify is the appetite of systems that cannot stop consuming.

WOE OVER THE CITY

Enoch's journeys: maps of heaven and the moral order of the world

Enoch is not a passive messenger. He is taken on tours through the cosmic architecture: storehouses of wind, the place where the waters begin, pillars that hold up the firmament, the gates where the sun rises and sets, the garden of righteousness, fragrant with trees of life, and the caverns of Sheol with separate compartments for the just and the unjust. These are not travelogues for curiosity; they are maps of moral geography. Reward and retribution are real, but not cartoonish. The righteous souls wait in luminous chambers; the violent and the slanderous await correction in shadowed hollows; the unrepentant receive what their deeds have chosen.

The Astronomical Book: a calendar with teeth

One of the most surprising sections of 1 Enoch is mathematical. The Astronomical Book meticulously describes the journey of the sun and moon through twelve portals, sets a 364-day solar calendar with four perfect quarters of ninety-one days, and synchronizes festivals to unerring cycles. Why the obsession? Because time is power. A community aligned to a precise calendar can order its worship without being jerked around by lunar irregularities or political manipulation. The calendar becomes an act of resistance, a pledge that the cosmos is intelligible and that sacred rhythms do not belong to kings.

The 364-day calendar in one minute

Four quarters, each with three months; the first and third months are thirty days, the second is thirty-one; four quarter-days mark the year's turn; festivals anchor to fixed weekdays; the result is an elegant schematic that preaches order.

The Parables: when Enoch meets the Son of Man

If the Watchers explain the disease, the Parables describe the cure. Here we meet the mysterious figure called the Son of Man, also titled the Elect One and the Righteous One. He is preeminent, enthroned beside the Ancient of Days, and tasked to judge kings and lift the oppressed. He is not a vague symbol; he acts. Mountains melt before him; those who exploited the poor tremble; the faithful are vindicated. The Parables are the thunderhead out of which the lightning of later messianic hope will strike. They give early readers a vocabulary for a personal agent of divine justice who is both humanly designated and transcendent in dignity.

This is the section that scandalizes and fascinates in equal measure, because it feels close to later Christian claims, yet it stands from within Jewish apocalyptic vision. Whatever your theology, recognize the essential promise: injustice is not permanent, arrogance is not immortal, and mercy is not weakness. History bends toward a judgment that is not blind.

SON
OF MAN

THE ANCIENT OF DAYS
AND SON OF MAN
Daniel 7 & Revelation 4-5

Dream Visions: history told with animals

Enoch dreams in symbols. In the Animal Apocalypse, nations and epochs become animals. Adam is a white bull; Israel is are sheep; oppressive empires appear as predators; the flood becomes a tidal purge; a future restoration arrives as the birth of a final white bull whose horns touch the sky. Do not press every symbol to yield an exact date. Feel the pedagogy. The vision distills the moral memory of a people: creation, fall, election, oppression, revolt, desecration, hope. When image and ethics align, communities endure.

Animal Apocalypse

The Epistle of Enoch: ethics after apocalyptic

Prophecy is not an escape hatch; it is a summons to character. The Epistle addresses sons and generations with stark counsel: flee injustice; do not love what fades; do not envy the wicked who build houses of clay; remember the poor; remember your words will judge you. In the Apocalypse of Weeks, history unfolds in seven-day metaphors that warn and console. The point is simple: the God who orders the stars sees your ledger. If the Watchers showcase catastrophic boundary-breaking, the Epistle restores boundary-keeping as a daily discipline: tell the truth; use power to serve; keep festivals with clean hands; give alms; honor covenants.

Why Enoch was beloved, then lost

Enoch was treasured in many Jewish and early Christian circles because it explained Genesis 6 with moral seriousness, promised final justice, and offered a calendar that anchored community life. So why was it not canonized widely? The short answer is geography and gatekeeping. In Aramaic and Greek, Enoch circulated vigorously in the centuries around the time of Jesus. After wars and migrations, key linguistic communities shifted. Some synagogue and church leaders grew wary of its angelology and exotic tours. Over time, Western churches set it aside. In the East, particularly in Ethiopia, it remained beloved and canonical. Loss is often less a verdict on truth and more a story about who kept copying which scrolls when empires rose and fell.

Angels, names, and natures

Enoch knows angels by name, and that is deliberate because in ancient thought, names describe functions. Seven faithful archangels recur: Michael, champion and intercessor; Gabriel, herald and warrior; Raphael, healer and binder of demons; Uriel, light and cosmic teacher; Raguel, restorer of order; Sariel or Saraqael, guide and judge; Remiel, overseer of the righteous dead. Opposed stand the Watchers who betrayed their commission. Azazel's sin is not merely lust; it is the weaponization of knowledge. Shemihazah's sin is not merely leadership; it is the vow that drags many down. Enoch's taxonomy teaches that evil is often hierarchical and technical, wrapped in expertise, and that the cure is courage joined to transparency.

Second and Third Enoch: ascent, transformation, and the crown of Metatron

Later Enochic traditions extend the arc. In 2 Enoch, preserved in Slavonic, the patriarch journeys through ten heavens. He sees prisons for rebel stars, storerooms of snow and dew, and the throne where he receives luminous garments. He returns with commandments for his sons. The tone is priestly and philosophical. In 3 Enoch, a Hebrew mystical text, the transformation is bolder: Enoch becomes Metatron, a princely being called "the lesser YH," a staggering title in that literature, enthroned as chief scribe of the King. Here, the focus tilts toward the Temple of Heaven and the techniques of ascent. These expansions show how Enoch's story became a scaffold for later visionary practice: ascent as obedience, not thrill; knowledge as gift, not piracy.

After the flood: did giants return

Ancient readers wrestled with texts that speak of later giants, and legends sprouted around names like Og. Enoch's internal logic suggests lingering spiritual fallout rather than a reset of biology. The giants' bodies die; their spirits continue to agitate. That is why the ethical fight continues after the water recedes. You do not argue with bones; you train your loves. If your era is anxious about predation, that is not superstition; it is discernment. The violence of appetite can surface in every century with new clothes.

Secrets they do not want you to know: what is truly "forbidden" in Enoch

The sensational answer would be technologies hidden in vaults. The sober answer is more unsettling: the forbidden secret is that judgment belongs to God and his timing is not for sale; that boundary-keeping protects the weak; that justice will outlast empires; that sacred time can be kept without imperial permission; that "knowledge" which bypasses virtue is a trap; that the Son of Man figure in the Parables is not a theory, but a claim about authority. Tyrants and profiteers dislike books like Enoch, not because they contain occult spikes to hack reality, but because they equip ordinary communities with moral maps that resist capture.

Three hard takeaways

1. Power that crosses creaturely boundaries becomes predatory; resist it.
2. Calendars shape conscience; order your time with purpose.
3. Prophecy without ethics is counterfeit; keep your hands clean while you wait for justice.

How to read Enoch wisely today

Approach the text with three lenses at once. First, read it as ancient apocalyptic, a genre that dramatizes moral reality with symbols and journeys. Second, read it as theology in story form, where angels and calendars carry claims about God and creation. Third, read it as cultural critique: Enoch's complaints about weaponized beauty, corrupted expertise, and predatory appetite feel current because human temptation recycles. Keep your footing. Do not let the imagery turn you into a code-chaser or a relic-hunter. Let it turn you into a neighbor who knows exactly why boundaries matter, why truth-telling is revolutionary, and why hope is not naive.

The long shadow of Enoch in Christian imagination

Even readers who never heard of 1 Enoch have likely felt its shadow. The language of angels that sin, chains of gloomy darkness, the coming One who judges the proud, the righteous remnant comforted with promises of a new earth, the Lamb who opens books, the city that descends clear as crystal, the river of life flanked by healing trees, the final separation of the exploiters from the meek, and the insistence that words, calendars, and covenants all matter, these are symmetries between Enoch and later Christian Scripture. Influence is not simple causation; it is conversation across texts. Enoch sits in that conversation as an elder whose voice is sometimes thunder, sometimes math, sometimes a father's last letter.

Enoch and the ethics of knowledge

At every turn, Enoch warns about a particular pattern. Knowledge that sidesteps the Maker's design collapses into manipulation. That is why Azazel's curriculum is an indictment. Make beauty that blesses, not glamor that enslaves. Forge tools that cultivate, not weapons that devour. Study the skies to keep time and praise, not to calculate omens that justify abuse. Enoch does not reject learning; he sanctifies its purpose. That is the edge we need now. We can split atoms, edit genomes, and train algorithms that predict desire. Will we do it as Watchers or as wise stewards? The text pushes the question to your conscience, not your curiosity.

Conclusion: what Enoch asks of us

Enoch asks you to decide what kind of knowledge you honor. It asks you to organize your life by a sanctified calendar rather than by the market. It asks you to name evil when it dresses in expertise. It asks you to love justice before it is fashionable. It asks you to hope for judgment without becoming vindictive. It asks you to be unafraid of maps, whether cosmic or moral. It asks you to remember that the one who "walked with God" did not vanish into privacy; he became the scribe of the world.

Enoch teaches that heaven listens to cries from the ground, that time can be kept without tyrants, that power will be weighed, and that even the stars serve righteousness. That is not a secret you hoard. That is a future you practice.

Chapter 3:

The Gnostic Gospels – Secret teachings of Jesus and Mary Magdalene

You came here for what is underneath the familiar story, the part that flickers in the margins of Scripture and refuses to stay quiet. The Gnostic gospels are not a detour; they are a second doorway into the earliest Christian memory. Open them carefully, and you find Jesus teaching in private, Mary Magdalene speaking with authority, and disciples wrestling with whether wisdom can arrive in a voice they did not expect. When we read these texts together, not as curiosities but as witnesses, a vivid portrait appears: a Jesus who insists the Kingdom is within reach, and a Mary who understands that message so deeply that some of the men protest and others defend her.

This chapter moves through that portrait step by step: first, what these writings are and how they were found; second, what the Gospel of Mary says about the secret teaching and Mary's contested leadership; third, how the Gospel of Thomas preserves a stream of sayings focused on inner knowledge; fourth, how the Gospel of Truth frames salvation as the cure for ignorance. Along the way, we will pull the threads together into a clear view of the voice that runs through them all.

What makes a gospel "Gnostic," and why that label can confuse

"Gnostic" points to a focus on direct knowing, not mere information, but a recognition that changes how you live. These writings are not uniform, yet they share a conviction that ignorance, fear, and false desire keep people small and that Jesus came to wake people up to their origin and destiny. Some texts weave mythic language, some speak in parables, some present extended dialogues. None of them feels like a late fan fiction. They feel like serious attempts to remember Jesus in a different key: intensely ethical, relentlessly interior, and very practical about how to become whole.

The jar in the desert, and a library of forgotten voices

In 1945, near the Egyptian village of Nag Hammadi, a jar broken open by a local farmer yielded a cache of ancient codices written mainly in Sahidic Coptic. Among them, in Codex II, sat the Gospel of Thomas, a collection of 114 sayings rather than a narrative life, an early witness that reads like a workshop for the inner life rather than a chronology of events. The find was literally a library, copied centuries after the time of Jesus, yet preserving traditions that had circulated much earlier.

The codices are papyrus books, not scrolls, copied in clear hands and, in some cases, in the Subakhmimic dialect. The physical volumes are fourth century, the thought-world they preserve is much older. The discovery matters because, for the first time, we could hear these communities in their own words, not only through their critics.

The Gospel of Mary: a contested teacher and the way to stability

If you read only one Gnostic text to understand the secret teachings connected with Mary Magdalene, start with the Gospel of Mary. It is not a biography. It is an intense dialogue before and after Jesus departs, followed by an argument among disciples about whether Mary's teaching should be trusted. The recipients named in the text include Peter, Mary, Andrew, and Levi. The narrative addresses the nature of the cosmos and redemption, interprets Scripture, reminds the disciples of their true identity, and unfolds Mary's account of the soul's ascent. That ascent confronts powers that try to hold the soul down, and the path forward is presented as the acquisition of stability that cuts through confusion and fear.

The heart of the drama is not only the content of Mary's vision; it is the reaction to her. In the preserved debate, the men speak about her rather than to her. Andrew questions whether her words differ from what they already know. Peter challenges the very premise that the Savior would reveal anything privately to a woman. Levi counters Peter with force: the Savior knew Mary completely and loved her more than the other disciples, and therefore made her worthy to receive and to share what she learned. The narrative itself sides against attempts to silence her and for a criterion of leadership based on understanding rather than gender.

Mary's teaching centers on becoming a true Human Being, a phrase that signals the restoration of wholeness. In her explanation, she identifies the adversaries that destabilize the mind: Darkness, Desire, Ignorance, and Wrath, with wrath's seven manifestations. The point is not an esoteric map for its own sake. The point is learning to discern false reasoning, to align with divine reason, and to move through the forces that make you forget who you are. The destination is Rest in Silence, not as an escape, but as a joyful victory over inner turbulence.

The author's craft is deliberate. Mary speaks for a long stretch, the same length or longer than the dialogue with the Savior. The composition invites readers to compare Mary's voice with Jesus' voice and to see the continuity in what she learned. In that way, the work argues by form, not merely by statements, that Mary's grasp of the teaching is solid and that her presence belongs at the center.

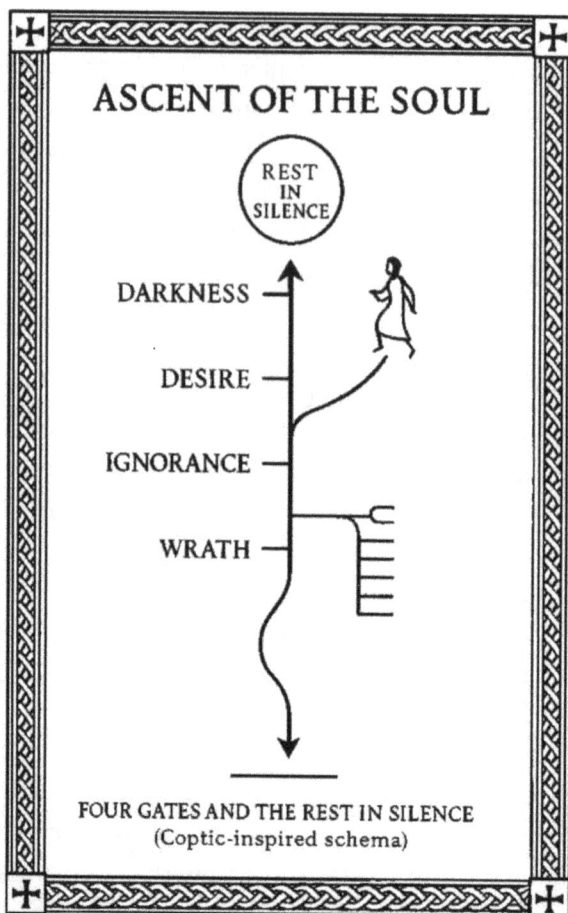

ASCENT OF THE SOUL

REST IN SILENCE

DARKNESS

DESIRE

IGNORANCE

WRATH

FOUR GATES AND THE REST IN SILENCE
(Coptic-inspired schema)

What the disciples argue about in the Gospel of Mary

Peter asserts Mary is preferred because she is a woman whom the Savior loved, then later rejects her teaching because she is a woman; Andrew doubts her because her teaching seems unfamiliar; Levi defends her, insisting the Savior made her worthy and loved her more than the others. The author frames the scene as a test of whether authority rests on gender or on depth of insight.

What the "secret" actually is

When Peter and Andrew object, they misread secrecy. The hiddenness is not elitism; it is about interiorization. The gospel in this text insists that your mind must stabilize, that you must learn to discern what comes from fear and what comes from knowing, that you must refuse to let wrath govern how you treat one another. Law and rule-making are introduced in the narrative precisely to critique the instinct to control others when you are afraid. Stability replaces control as the path to peace.

This is why the Gospel of Mary is not a tract about women only. It is an argument for egalitarian discipleship rooted in the capacity to illuminate the Savior's words. The author refutes those who dismiss Mary because she is a woman and presents a vision of leadership based on understanding, courage, and fidelity.

Mary and the canonical Gospels: how her teaching style fits the earliest memories

Across the New Testament, women often remind the men of what Jesus already said, especially around Easter. In John's account, uniquely, Mary receives new content and interprets it correctly on her own initiative. The Gospel of Mary aligns most closely with that Johannine pattern, showing Mary taught alone by Jesus, then sharing instruction with the others. The difference is that the Gospel of Mary makes the implicit debate explicit, staging the challenge and the defense so that readers cannot miss the stakes.

John depicts meaningful dialogues with women, though still within conservative boundaries; the Synoptics keep most women's voices offstage. The Gospel of Mary moves the conversation into full view and lets the audience watch the men decide whether they will accept correction from a woman whose understanding outstrips theirs.

The Gospel of Thomas: 114 sayings that train perception

Thomas is not a story; it is a set of 114 sayings attributed to Jesus. There are no miracle narratives, no passion chronicle. It reads like a spiritual practicum. The first audience would have known the public stories. Thomas offers the inner drill: attention, interpretation, and the move from scattered life to integrated life.

The tradition that produced Thomas understood Jesus as a teacher whose words could be lived into, not merely admired. It places the focus on becoming fully conscious, moving from limited perception to an expanded awareness of what is present. You can hear why this text was treasured alongside the public gospels. It preserves a voice that refuses to flatter or console. It aims to wake you up.

A brief note on discovery helps here. The book that preserves Thomas in Codex II is part of the same Nag Hammadi library found near the old Pachomian monasteries. The codices were copied in Coptic. The discovery opened a forceful new chapter in scholarship because it let researchers read non-canonical voices without a filter.

Thomas also explains why Mary's voice is plausible in early circles. The text cares less about official roles and more about who understands. That is the logic we saw in the Gospel of Mary: those who can interpret faithfully, those who stabilize the mind and embody the teaching, lead by substance rather than by title.

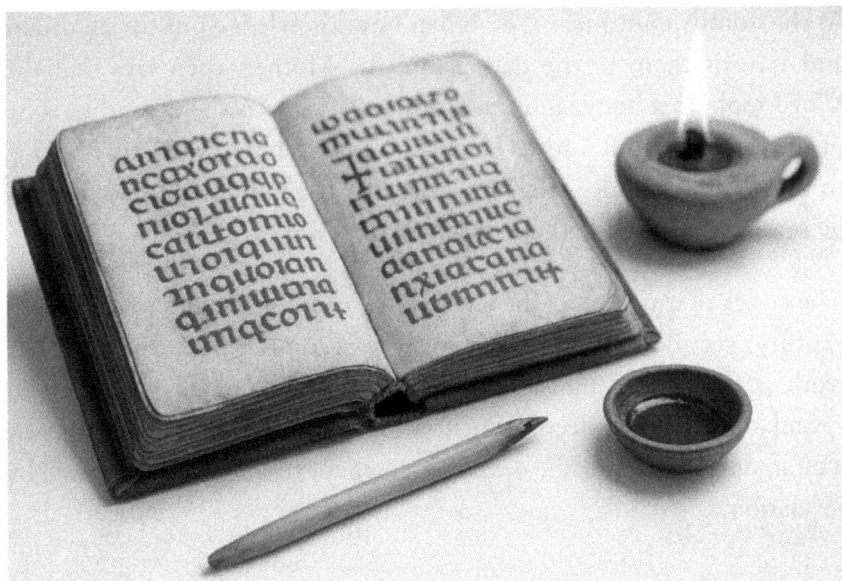

Coptic Leaves: Page, Pen, and Lamp

The Gospel of Truth: salvation as the cure of ignorance

Another text that illuminates the secret teaching is the Gospel of Truth, widely connected with the Valentinian school. Its structure is more homily than story. It begins with the claim that the good news is joy for all who come to know the Savior, and it identifies the core human problem as ignorance of the Father, which breeds fear and error. In this telling, Jesus brings knowledge that restores what ignorance has disordered.

The text narrates the crucifixion with striking images. Error, enraged at the Gnosis he brought, nailed him to the wood, and he became a fruit of the Father's knowledge. Those who eat of this fruit become joyful. The homily speaks of the book that only the one to be sacrificed can take, and the "book of the living" for those who receive the teaching. It is not myth for myth's sake; it is an insistence that revelation undoes terror.

As the homily continues, it describes how knowledge purifies all things and returns them to the Father and the Mother, then says that the Word took on a body, and that knowledge relieves the dreamlike state of those who do not know. The goal is unity. Those who truly belong to the Divine do not search anxiously for truth; they become truthful beings in whom the Father dwells.

The codex that transmits the Gospel of Truth likely dates to the fourth century, yet the thought it carries fits a second-century context. The work is frequently linked to Valentinus or his circle, not as a wild speculation, but as a deeply Christian meditation that reveres the New Testament's witness while developing a theology of ignorance cured by revelation.

The arc of the Gospel of Truth in one line

Ignorance fostered fear and error, the Son revealed knowledge, the cross is depicted as public fruit that cures oblivion, and the end is unity with the Father through a life that becomes truth.

Mary Magdalene as disciple, interpreter, and model of stability

Across several early writings, Mary appears not only as a symbol but as a working disciple. In the Gospel of Mary, she encourages the others when they are afraid, interprets the Savior's words, and lays out the ascent of the soul past the personified adversaries that confuse and entrap. The author gives her as much room to speak as to Jesus, a structural signal that her understanding is the correct one and the one the community is meant to follow.

Within the narrative, four male positions about her teaching are put in play and weighed. The one that wins is the one that measures by understanding, not by sex. That outcome dovetails with the claim that the gospel is entrusted to any disciple who can shed light on the teaching. It is not a manifesto; it is an argument crafted in a story.

In the broader New Testament comparison, this makes sense. John already depicts Mary learning alone from Jesus and announcing something new. The Gospel of Mary intensifies that memory and sets it where no reader can miss it: inside a community debate about whether to listen to her.

The content of the "secret teaching": how to become a true Human Being

Now to the core theme that ties these texts together. The secret is not a list of passwords; it is a program for becoming whole. In the Gospel of Mary, the inner adversaries are named so you can notice them when they rise in you. Darkness, Desire, Ignorance, and Wrath do not only describe cosmic powers; they describe the real states that pull people away from good sense and courage. Mary's teaching is practical: discern false reasoning, ally with divine reason, and learn stability. The destination is a Rest that is also action, the calm that lets you speak up, reconcile, and endure.

The Gospel of Truth says the same thing in a different register. Human beings sleepwalk through life, not because they are bad, but because they do not know where they came from. When the knowledge of the Father arrives, it is like sobering up from drunkenness; it is like daylight after a long night. The cross becomes fruit that reverses the lie that death and fear tell. The result is unity: nerves settled, vision clear, courage restored.

Thomas adds the drill. It puts 114 sayings in your hands and tells you to keep listening until you hear the tone beneath the words. Many of those sayings are abrasive on purpose because they are meant to interrupt habits that keep you asleep. They do not ask for blind faith. They ask for attention and for a readiness to let go of borrowed identities.

Why the argument about Mary mattered then, and why it matters now

If the Gospel of Mary only told us that a woman once spoke up, it would be inspiring but limited. It does more. It shows a community deciding what counts as authority. Andrew says new content should be rejected because it is unfamiliar. Peter says gender disqualifies. Levi says Jesus knew Mary perfectly and honored her insight, so the community should do the same. The author clearly favors Levi. The point is not to score a win for one faction; the point is to show readers how to weigh voices in their own communities. Knowledge that produces stability and courage is the credential that matters.

The same lens helps us read the canonical Gospels more shrewdly. They are androcentric in different ways. The Synoptics often have women present but silent. John gives them meaningful words, yet keeps them within tight social bounds. The Gospel of Mary exposes the dynamic that those texts imply and makes the stakes explicit. It honors Mary not as a token, but as a teacher who steadies faltering hearts and shows them how to move forward.

PRACTICE OF GNOSIS

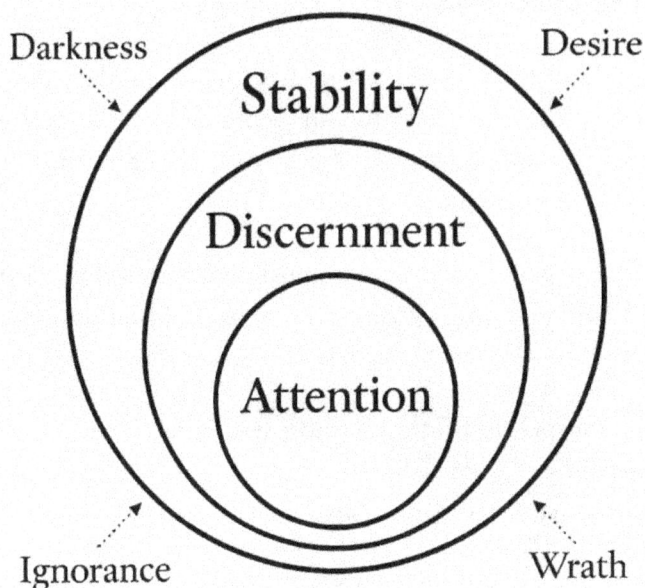

Darkness

Desire

Stability

Discernment

Attention

Ignorance

Wrath

Distractions to be recognized:
Darkness, Desire, Ignorance, Wrath

How the pieces fit: a single thread through different voices

Lay the three texts side by side and watch the thread:

1. The Gospel of Mary, the most explicit on Mary's authority, teaches that the true Human Being emerges when the mind learns to stand firm. It dramatizes a community choosing insight over prejudice.

2. The Gospel of Thomas, the most concentrated in form, trains perception through sayings that insist on inner transformation. It does not flatter the reader; it expects growth.

3. The Gospel of Truth, the most homiletic, heals ignorance by proclaiming knowledge as a divine gift, and reimagines the cross as fruit that cures oblivion.

Together, they do exactly what a good teacher does: they name your obstacles, give you practice in seeing clearly, and anchor you in a story where fear no longer rules your decisions.

Addressing common objections with clarity

Objection one: These writings are too late to matter. Response: The codices are fourth century, yet they preserve material whose style and concerns fit the second century, and in the case of Thomas, many sayings parallel early traditions in form and tone. The value is not in pretending these are first-hand stenographic records, but in reading them as serious early Christian reflections that draw from streams known to the earliest communities.

Objection two: Gnosis sounds elitist.

Response: In these texts, the opposite is true. Knowledge is not secret information; it is the recognition that cures fear and false desire. The Gospel of Truth is explicit that ignorance produces terror and division, and that the Savior reveals knowledge to deliver people from that state. In the Gospel of Mary, leadership is measured by who can stabilize the mind and build the community up, not who can guard a mystery for the few.

Objection three: Mary's prominence must be an invention to serve a later agenda.

Response: The New Testament itself preserves lines that make Mary's role plausible, especially in John, where she receives instruction alone and announces the core resurrection message. The Gospel of Mary magnifies that thread and clarifies a debate that the canonical texts leave in the background.

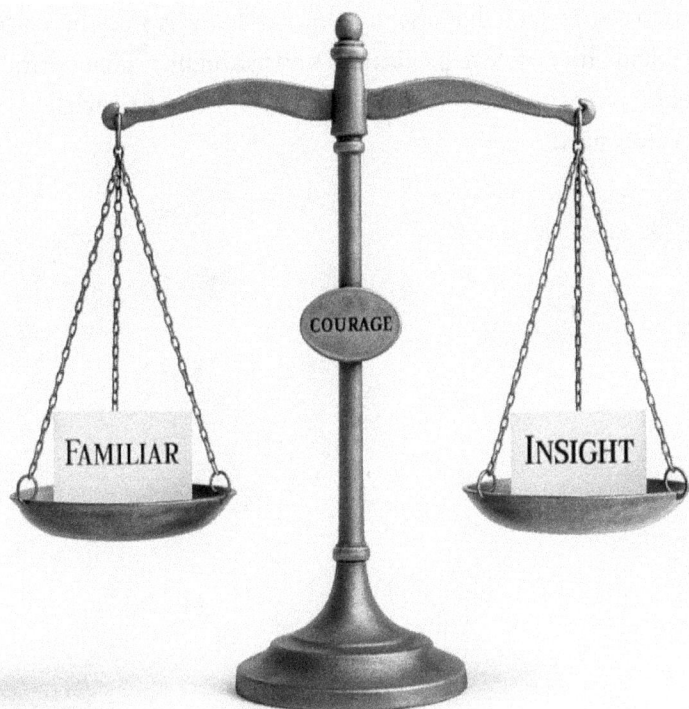

Practical takeaways

First, pay attention to the training these texts propose. Stability is not passivity; it is readiness. The way Mary names the adversaries helps anyone diagnose the states that make them reactive. Learning to spot Wrath with its many faces, learning to catch Ignorance before it hardens into contempt, frees a person to act with clarity. That is as useful in a family dispute as it is in a congregation.

Second, test the authority by fruit. In the Gospel of Mary, the person who steadies the fearful, interprets the Master accurately, and sends the group into its mission is the one to trust. The story does not tell you to despise institutions; it tells you to look for leadership that produces courage and peace.

Third, let the cross become fruit again. The Gospel of Truth's image is not decorative. It says that the sign of suffering is not the endpoint; what looked like defeat becomes nourishment. That shift cures resentment and restores hope, which is exactly what divided communities need.

Trellis & Text

A note on method: reading without fear of depth

To make the most of these sources, read them in conversation with the canonical gospels rather than against them. The earliest communities did not live with the neat categories later centuries prefer. They told stories, preserved sayings, preached, debated, edited, and copied. In that dynamic, texts like Mary, Thomas, and Truth remain valuable because they show real Christians wrestling with what Jesus meant and how to live it. They are not "winners" or "losers" in a competition. They are witnesses to the power that lifted ordinary people out of fear.

That is why the Gospel of Mary ends the way it does: with the disciples deciding to go out and preach. Not because everyone agreed about everything, but because the teaching had stabilized their minds and set their purpose. It is a scene that feels very human and very familiar.

Threshold: Into the Daylight

Read together, the Gnostic gospels are not distractions from the story; they are part of it. They preserve a Jesus who insists that what you need is nearer than you think, and a Mary who learned that lesson so well that she could teach it back to the others when they wavered. The secret is not scandal, it is the quiet courage that comes when ignorance gives way to knowledge and fear gives way to love. That is what these texts are guarding. That is the part of the Bible's history that is only forbidden if we forbid ourselves to look.

If you let that thread run through you, you will understand why these writings were done with care, why they traveled in a clay jar across centuries, and why their counsel still steadies people who choose to listen.

One sentence to carry with you

Measure every claim of authority in the church by the same test these texts apply: does it cure ignorance, quiet wrath, and send people out with courage and peace; if so, trust it, if not, look again.

Chapter 4:

Apocalypses They Tried to Erase – Peter, Hermas, and visions of the end

If you want to understand why certain books rose to the top of Christian memory while others were buried, hidden, or quietly set aside, follow the trail of visions. Early Christians loved visions, they argued over visions, and they built their hope for the future on visions. Yet the apocalypses that did not fit the emerging consensus, or that kept inconvenient kinds of authority alive, were trimmed away. This chapter takes you straight into two of the most revealing survivors of that pruning: the Apocalypse of Peter and the Shepherd of Hermas. One shows you divine judgment with unnerving specificity, the other insists that time remains for repentance, then reminds you that time is nearly up. Together they map an early Christian battlefield: Who speaks for the risen Christ, what counts as revelation, and how does the world end?

Before we step into those texts, set the stage. From the late first century through the third, Christian groups produced revelatory books in the idiom of Jewish apocalyptic: a seer receives heavenly disclosure through an angel or through the risen Jesus, often in the form of a tour, a dialogue, or a symbolic drama. Canonical Revelation is the best known, but it was never alone. Visionary gospels and dialogues circulated widely, and collections preserved them for communities that prized revelation as much as doctrine. The chance discovery of a jar full of Coptic books near Nag Hammadi in Upper Egypt revealed how vigorous and diverse that literature was, right down to a competing Apocalypse of Peter with a very different Christology. The find was literally a library dug out of the sand, a fourth-century codex set that had preserved voices that official memory left out.

Why apocalypses were risky

Revelation confers authority. In a movement that insists the risen Christ continues to teach, whoever claims to have seen and heard can claim to lead. That made visionary texts powerful, and it made them dangerous. You can watch the tension play out in post-Easter dialogues where one disciple recounts a private vision and another questions it. A vivid example is the clash between Peter and Mary in a gospel that survived in Coptic fragments. Mary recounts the Lord's words from a vision. Peter challenges her legitimacy, not only as a visionary but as a woman, and another disciple rebukes him, reminding the group that if the Savior made her worthy, none of them should silence her. The scene captures a recurring early-Christian argument: Does the risen Christ speak only through public, male, apostolic lines, or can private visions, even by women, instruct the whole group?

That lived tension matters when you evaluate the fate of Peter's apocalypse and Hermas's visions. Neither text vanishes because it is boring. Each carries a claim about how Christ governs his church in the last days, and how the end will meet the present.

The Apocalypse of Peter: a guided tour of judgment, and a scandal of mercy

There are two texts with this title, and you should keep them straight.

What to notice in visionary disputes

- The form: a seer narrates a private dialogue with the risen Jesus, then other disciples interrogate the claim.
- The stakes: who teaches, who leads, and what counts as "from the Lord."
- The outcome: sometimes reconciliation, sometimes a split in memory.

1. An early second-century apocalypse attributed to Peter circulated in Greek and Ethiopic. It stages a heavenly tour in which Jesus shows Peter the punishments of the wicked and the blessedness of the righteous. The structure is simple to follow: Peter asks, the Lord answers, and a series of vivid tableaux unfolds. The moral logic is strict: torments often mirror the sin. The voice of Jesus, however, is not only a judge's, it is also the tour guide who interprets what Peter sees. That format made the work powerful for preaching and catechesis. People recognized the voice and the visuals.

2. A different work, preserved in a Coptic codex from Upper Egypt, also bears the title Apocalypse of Peter. In this one, the risen Christ reveals to Peter that the crucifixion was not what it appeared to be. The living Jesus stands above the cross, calm and laughing, while a substitute body suffers below. The point is not mockery; it is a metaphysical claim: blind powers crucify what they can grasp, the outer form, while the true, living one remains untouchable. You can feel how dramatically this vision departs from the emerging consensus that insisted on a real passion and a bodily resurrection. That is why this version remained in a desert library rather than in a church lectionary. The very existence of such alternative apocalypses, preserved together in codices, is part of what the Nag Hammadi discovery brought to light.

Why the early church hesitated

The church did not reject the early Apocalypse of Peter simply because it was lurid. Leaders read and cited it. Some lists allowed it to be read, but not in public worship, which is a crucial distinction. The problems were these.

- First, the text's pastoral utility came with a risk. A graphic tour of punishments can slide from moral exhortation into sensationalism. If a congregation comes to crave spectacles of torment, you have lost the point of judgment, which is conversion.

- Second, a strand of the tradition attached to the work hinted at a final mercy that reaches even those in punishment. That possibility, reported by respected teachers in antiquity, did not sit easily with the hardening outlines of doctrine. The tension was never fully resolved. In some manuscripts, the mercy note is subdued or absent. Where it remained audible, it was too bright for gatekeepers who wanted the line between the saved and the lost to stand fast.

- Third, the authority claim mattered. A Petrine apocalypse could rival Revelation not only in theme but in voice. You can affirm Peter as an apostle while still deciding that his vision is not for public reading, and that is precisely what many churches did.

What makes it distinctive

The tour format functions like a catechism through images. The righteous are recognizable not by tribal identity but by acts of mercy, justice, and patient endurance. The condemned are named by the harm they inflicted on others. The seer asks questions many churchgoers still ask: Will wrongs be put right? Will hidden crimes come into the light? Shall we ever see the world judged by a fair standard? The apocalypse answers yes, then shows you how.

The Shepherd of Hermas: visions, mandates, and the last construction deadline

If Peter's apocalypse is a tour, Hermas is a course. A Roman Christian named Hermas receives five visions, twelve mandates, and ten parables, all delivered by an angelic figure called the Shepherd. The drama is not a cosmic battle; it is construction management. The church appears as an old woman who grows younger as people repent, or as a tower under construction whose stones represent believers. Each image teaches what time it is and what to do next.

The key themes are bracing.

One repentance after baptism: Hermas insists that there remains room, once, for return after grave failure. That discipline is not lenient; it is merciful without being naïve. It combats despair without condoning drift.

Wealth and worry: The visions target the moral hazard of prosperity. Rich Christians can become dead weight in the tower, brittle branches that look fine, then snap under stress. Hermas offers a reallocation plan: share generously, release debts, and stand with the poor. That is how the tower rises.

Testing and delay: A monstrous beast threatens, the ground shakes, and then the Shepherd announces that the end is put off for a short season, precisely to allow repentance. The point is not to feed speculation about dates. The point is to decide on the present. The tower is nearly finished. Bring your stone or step aside.

Why did this not make the canon, given how widely the book was read and copied? Ironically, because it was so popular and so recent. Communities loved it, scribes preserved it with Scripture in major codices, and respected leaders found it useful. At the same time, the push to define an apostolic canon tightened the criteria. The book was edifying, even authoritative in practice, but it lacked an apostolic name and felt too close to their own time. So it lived at the church's elbow rather than its heart. That is what it means when a text keeps showing up in Christian codices yet is labeled "for reading," not "for reading in the assembly." It was not erased. It was benched.

How Hermas imagines the end

- The end is near enough to motivate, yet delayed for mercy.
- Judgment is visible now in the quality of your life, not only later in crisis.
- The church is a project, not a club: you bring your stone and your labor.

Peter and Hermas in conversation

Set the two alongside one another, and the picture sharpens.

Audience and tone: Peter speaks in images designed to shake the conscience, Hermas in instructions designed to form it. One aims at fear rightly ordered, the other at hope rightly disciplined.

Visions and authority: Both texts frame their claim through a divinely guided seer. Attach the name Peter to a guided tour of judgment, and you have a rival to Revelation that draws on apostolic gravitas. Place an angelic Shepherd at the side of a Roman layman, and you democratize revelation, not by trivializing it, but by making accountability the measure of authenticity. That democratization would later make gatekeepers nervous, given how revelation can be used to bypass settled leadership.

Judgment and mercy: Peter's work, in some forms, whispers that mercy may reach farther than people think. Hermas shouts that mercy is real, then sets a hard deadline. Both stabilize a community torn between despair and presumption.

The end itself: Neither text treats the end as a calendar curiosity. The end is the moment when God's truth finally runs through everything. Peter dramatizes that moment. Hermas drills people for it. The practical effect is the same: live now as if the world were about to be weighed.

How these apocalypses nearly made it, then did not

To see why these books were "almost Scripture," trace their life cycle.

1. **Birth in crisis:** They arise when persecution, betrayal, wealth, and delay test Christian communities. People demand to know if the world is still governed and if Christ is still speaking.

2. **Rapid adoption:** The texts circulate. They are copied with Scripture, read aloud, and used for instruction. In some places, Peter's apocalypse is known well enough that teachers comment on it. In others, Hermas becomes the go-to handbook for penitents and sponsors.

3. **Boundary setting:** As leaders define a public set of books for worship, the question narrows from "Is this edifying?" to "Is this apostolic and universal?" Works like Hermas receives a respectful no. Works like the Petrine apocalypse receives a cautious no. The reasons include theology, date, and perceived risk.

4. **Long afterlife:** Neither text disappears. They keep teaching, often just outside the liturgy. They shape imagination. They influence preaching on judgment, repentance, wealth, and hope.

That outcome sits within a broader pattern. The second and third centuries generate a spectrum of revelatory texts: visionary gospels, post-resurrection dialogues, and apocalyptic tours. The library found near Nag Hammadi reminds us that entire communities treasured this spectrum, even when church leaders elsewhere narrowed it. That discovery, told so often that it has become a modern origin story, matters because it reveals how much ancient Christians copied, bound, and hid rather than burned.

The contested right to see

Return to that early dialogue where Mary reports a vision, Peter protests, and another disciple tells Peter to stand down. The scene is not gossip; it is a mirror. The authority to interpret the end is the authority to interpret the present. When someone says, "I saw the Lord and this is what it means for us," the community must decide how to weigh the claim. The earliest Christians did not pretend the risen Christ had gone silent. They argued about how to test the voices.

Two details are crucial.

Visions come with instruction, not only spectacle. In Mary's case, the Lord teaches about the discipline of the mind that sees. In Hermas the Shepherd assigns mandates. In Peter, the Lord explains the moral logic behind the scenes of judgment. Revelatory texts that last do more than amaze. They catechize.

Disputes center on legitimacy, not curiosity. Peter's pushback against Mary in that dialogue is not about the content alone; it is about whether a woman can speak for the Lord. That tells you how social order and revelation intertwine. Communities that feared an open pipeline from the risen Christ to any believer also feared chaos. Communities that trusted the pipeline feared ossification. That is why visionary books rise and fall with debates about who may teach.

Where Nag Hammadi helps, and where it does not

A word about what modern discoveries actually do. The codices from Upper Egypt preserved a different Apocalypse of Peter, a sayings gospel attributed to Thomas with no end-time narrative, and several post-resurrection dialogues. As a set, they reveal that early Christians copied and kept visionary and revelatory books even when they did not fit the emerging canon. That matters for our chapter because it shows how normal it was to explore revelation through dialogues and visions. It also shows how diverse the Christologies around those visions were. In some works, the risen Jesus laughs above the instruments of death. In others, he commissions harsh judgment. In still others, he teaches inward watchfulness rather than an outward timetable. Those books were hidden, not because Christians had an allergy to visions, but because they had to choose which visions would anchor public worship and doctrine.

Apocalypses that survived the winnowing survived because they teach people how to end well. Peter's apocalypse ends by forcing you to look at your life through God's eyes. Hermas ends by forcing you to move while there is still time. The vision withers if you only admire it. It ripens if you act. That is why some people tried to erase these books. Not because they could not understand them, but because they understood exactly what such visions demand.

And that returns us to the question of authority. Who gets to say what the risen Christ demands today? The early church answered by listening widely, arguing plainly, and finally choosing a common set of books for common worship. Even then, communities kept a shelf for texts like Peter and Hermas, books that keep the conscience awake.

Part II — Secrets Unearthed

Chapter 5: The Dead Sea Scrolls – Hidden Wisdom of the Essenes

If you want to understand how bold, how strange, and how disciplined a small desert movement can be, start in the limestone cliffs above the Dead Sea. There, in caves cut by wind and time, a cache of ancient manuscripts slept for two millennia. When the first jars were opened in the late 1940s, scholars realized they were looking at something unmatched in biblical studies: the oldest large collection of Hebrew manuscripts on earth, copied by a separatist community that called itself the Yahad, the unity. This chapter is a guided walk through those caves, the settlement below them, and the ideas that shaped the people who likely stored those scrolls. We will keep the story practical and grounded: what the texts actually say, how the site functioned, where the debates still are, and why the Essenes matter for anyone who cares about the Bible and the birth of early Christianity.

The discovery, the site, and the library

Between 1947 and 1956, Bedouin shepherds and archaeologists explored eleven caves near Khirbet Qumran on the northwest shore of the Dead Sea. They pulled out more than nine hundred manuscripts in Hebrew, Aramaic, and a little Greek. Some jars held nearly complete rolls, others only crumbly scraps. The manuscripts ranged from biblical books to community rules, hymns, legal letters, commentaries, and a few surprises that resist easy labels. The caves overlook a plateau scattered with the ruins of a communal compound that flourished in the first centuries before and after the turn of the era.

The site itself has been excavated in multiple seasons since the 1950s. The basic picture is clear: long halls, multiple ritual baths, water channels, workshops, and a large dining assembly space. Exactly how to label the site is debated. Many scholars see a sectarian center that managed a library and practiced strict purity. Others stress military and industrial features that echo a small fortress, noting that one interpretation does not exclude the other. What is not debated is the importance of the library stored in the caves, a library that shows the convictions and internal debates of a desert movement that read Scripture with fierce intensity.

Who were the Essenes, and why does Qumran look like them

Three ancient writers, independent of each other, describe a Jewish sect called Essenes. One was a statesman and historian who defected to Rome, one a philosopher in Alexandria, and one a Roman naturalist. They agree on core traits: communal property, strict admission procedures, a reputation for purity and truthfulness, and a disciplined daily rhythm centered on study, prayer, and shared meals. The scrolls and the site fit this profile with unusual precision: communal meals blessed by priests, property under communal oversight, probationary periods, ritual baths, and a distinctive reading of biblical law.

priests

pantry
with stacked
vessels

Qumran Communal Dining Hall (Refectory), Late Second
Temple Period

What the scrolls are, in plain terms

Open the archive and you will find several kinds of writings. Here is a
quick map of the ones we will draw on most.

1. **Community Rule, 1QS**: a constitution for admission,
   discipline, communal meals, liturgy, and authority. It defines
   ranks, spells out penalties, and lays down the ethos: truth,
   humility, and separation from a corrupt outside. Surviving
   copies show editorial layers, but the heart is clear, a manual for
   life together under priestly oversight.

2. **Thanksgiving Hymns, Hodayot:** personal poems that sound like the Psalms filtered through a desert conscience. The speaker confesses human frailty, thanks God for revealed knowledge, and celebrates being rescued from "the lot of darkness."

3. **Pesharim, commentaries:** verse-by-verse interpretations, especially on prophets like Habakkuk. These are not ordinary commentaries. They decode Scripture as a live script for current events, naming a Teacher of Righteousness and his enemies.

4. **War Scroll, 1QM:** a field manual for the last battles, with trumpet calls, troop rotations, priestly blessing formulas, and a cosmic enemy called the Sons of Darkness. This is apocalyptic liturgy more than logistics, yet it shows how the movement imagined its role in history.

5. **Temple Scroll:** the longest scroll, a sweeping legal blueprint that rewrites and amplifies biblical law in God's voice, as if Sinai were being specified again for a purer temple and city. It moves from inner courts outward and knits festivals, sacrificial procedures, and purity laws into a vision of ideal worship.

6. **Damascus Document:** a rule text preserved both in the Cairo Genizah and at Qumran, outlining covenant theology, leadership, and discipline. It links the movement to an earlier split with mainstream priests and offers a history of their own group's calling.

7. **Copper Scroll:** unique for its medium and content, it lists dozens of hidden caches of silver and gold with coordinates that read like a treasure map. Its language and date set it apart from other sectarian works, and the big question remains whether it records real deposits or something else entirely.

Inside the Community Rule: admissions, meals, and morals

The Rule opens with a covenant ceremony. Candidates confess in public that they have joined the lot of light. Admission is slow and costly. Prospects surrender property to the treasury, but it is held in trust during probation. They eat separately until fully admitted. Penalties are precise, often measured in days of exclusion from communal meals or demotion in rank. The Rule sets priests at the head of the table and in charge of blessing the bread and wine. The structure is tight, yet the ideal is ethical as much as ritual: truth in speech, humility, mutual correction, and care for the poor in their midst. The Rule even anticipates disagreement, insisting that the overseer, a key officer, weigh cases carefully and teach daily.

Calendars and purity: the pressure points

Two issues drove a permanent wedge between the movement and the Jerusalem establishment. First, the calendar. The group followed a 364-day solar scheme that fixed festivals on the same weekday every year. That meant their Pentecost and other feasts never matched the lunar calendar used by the priests in the city. Second, purity standards. The scrolls articulate a high wall of separation regarding the temple, tithes, marriage, and bodily fluids. These were not minor lifestyle choices. They were boundary markers that defined the community as Israel in microcosm, true Israel in exile.

The War Scroll: a liturgy of battle

The War Scroll is famous for phrases like Sons of Light and Sons of Darkness. Read closely, it is a priestly book of war. Priests bless the shields. Trumpets signal charges. There are detailed rotations for six and seven-year cycles, and formulae for victory hymns. It is less of a war diary and more of a blueprint for a sacred campaign that God will finally win, with the community's purity treated as a weapon. You hear echoes of the Rule: order, rank, blessing, separation.

Pesharim: how the Essenes read the prophets

If you have ever listened to someone say, "This verse is happening now," you already understand pesher. The commentaries on Habakkuk and other prophets treat Scripture as a sealed code that needs a teacher to open it. Names are masked with titles. The Teacher of Righteousness is contrasted with the Wicked Priest and the Man of Lies. The method is consistent: quote a line, then explain how it maps onto current figures and events. This reveals what mattered to them: God's timetable, the corruption of the city, the vindication of their Teacher, and a conviction that they stood in the last act of Israel's story.

וַיַּעֲנֵנִי יְהוָה

כְּזוֹב רְאָמֶר *interpretation*

הַבָּזוֹן עַל־חוֹת

לְמַעַץ קוֹרָא בּוֹ

Write the Vision
Habakkuk 2:2 (Masoretic Text)

The Temple Scroll: rewriting Sinai for a perfect city

The Temple Scroll is written as divine speech. That alone tells you the stakes. It specifies the ideal temple precinct, radiating outward, and ties each zone to purity rules, sacrificial schedules, and festival rhythms. It reads like an architect's directive married to a law code. This is not fantasy. It is a legal claim. The movement believed that a malformed temple in Jerusalem polluted the people, so they kept a new temple ready on paper.

Modern science has probed even the material of this scroll. Researchers studied its salts and collagen and showed how its thin, bright parchment was manufactured in a distinctive way, which helps conservators and also underlines that the Temple Scroll really is an outlier physically among the corpus.

Copper, not parchment: the puzzle scroll

The Copper Scroll lists scores of deposits of gold and silver with astonishing specificity. It is singular in material, tone, and perhaps purpose. Some read it as a real inventory of temple assets hidden during the war. Others think it is a memory list, a didactic exercise, or a claim about legitimized wealth. No one has recovered its treasures. What is valuable beyond speculation is the window it offers into the financial imagination of the period and the broader geography it assumes.

Law as a dividing line: the Halakhic Letter

A text known by its initials, MMT, sets out legal disagreements on purity and offerings. What matters is not only the rulings but the rhetorical frame. The writers appeal to their addressees to join them in correct practice, implying a crack with the temple. These positions line up in places with views later attributed to Sadducees, which has led some to argue that the community began as a priestly reform aligned with that party. Others reply that the document is not sectarian or that overlaps do not erase Essene identity. Either way, MMT is vital because it shows how a calendar and a handful of ritual details can create a complete social separation.

Archaeology meets text: latrines, waterworks, and a scribal room.

The compound's elaborate water channels feed multiple stepped pools. These are not for leisure. They are ritual baths for immersion, and their number and volume match the Rule's obsession with purity. Excavators noted a long room with inkwells and benches that fit a scriptorium, the place where texts could be copied. Even the location of latrines outside the camp line up with a biblical reading the group embraced, a small but telling detail that shows how the site and the scrolls reinforce each other. Debate remains over whether the site began as a fortress and then became sectarian. The most sensible reading allows both, with a later sect adapting an older military footprint.

Qumran Core Complex (Loci 77 & 30) – Clean Plan

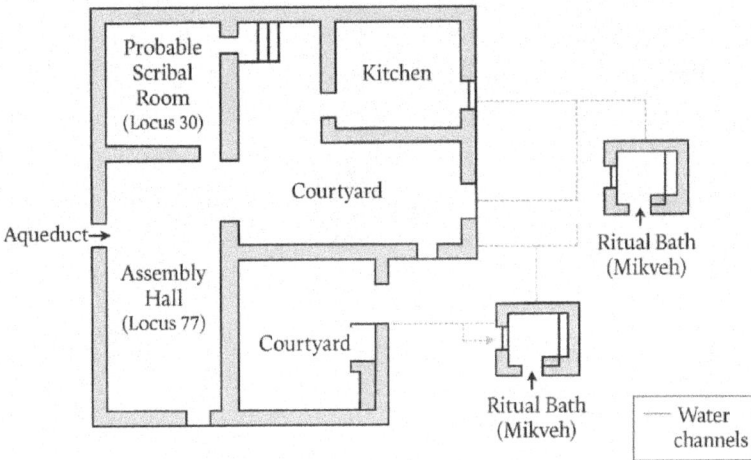

Assembly Hall, Kitchen, Mikva'ot, and Water Channels

What the scrolls did for the Bible you read.

The biblical manuscripts at Qumran are older than the medieval copies that underlie most printed Bibles. They show that multiple textual traditions circulated, sometimes side by side, before a later standardization. The famous Isaiah scroll, for example, is astonishingly close to the later Masoretic tradition in many places, yet there are meaningful differences. Other books exist in forms that echo the Greek translation or the Samaritan edition. The point is simple and powerful: Scripture had a living textual history, and the scrolls let you see it breathing.

Digital projects now let you zoom into the fibers of these parchments and compare readings at your desk. For a subject that once required a flight and a white glove, this accessibility has democratized study and forced arguments to be made on evidence rather than mystique.

New tools, new questions: DNA and radiocarbon

Ancient DNA from the parchment itself has been used to cluster fragments by the animal they came from, helping scholars decide which scraps belong together and which do not. This is not a parlor trick. It has resolved real puzzles, clarified when different copies of the same work came from different herds, and flagged imports into the region. Cleaning methods and improved radiocarbon sampling have also redated some pieces, reminding everyone to hold earlier assumptions lightly, especially when conservation oils applied in the 1950s skewed results.

What kind of spirituality is this

If you read the Thanksgiving Hymns aloud, a tone emerges. It is not swagger. It is not despair. It is a disciplined humility that attributes insight to divine revelation and weakness to human limits. The Rule's ethics mirror that tone: honesty, mutual rebuke without cruelty, generosity to the needy within the camp, and a dislike of slander. The group resists divorce, regulates sexuality, and imposes social ranks. This is not abstract mysticism. It is embodied piety.

How Essene ideas overlap with early Christianity, and how they do not

There are family resemblances worth noticing. Both the Essenes and the earliest Christians practiced communal meals with blessings over bread and wine from a priestly or leadership figure. Both were baptized, although the meanings and settings differ. Both interpreted Scripture as a present word. Both expected God to act soon and decisively. Both cultivated charity and a rigorous moral code.

There are also deep differences. The Essenes withdrew to purify themselves, applied law in maximalist fashion, and envisioned two messiahs, priestly and royal, who would restore an ideal temple calendar and cult. The early Christian movement was temple-positive at first, then became a portable community centered on the risen Jesus, opening membership across ethnic lines without adopting the Essene calendar or purity walls. Reading both together, you come away with a clearer sense of the Jewish landscape into which Jesus and John the Baptist spoke.

The Teacher of Righteousness, the Wicked Priest, and history on a knife-edge

The pesharim outline a story that many reconstruct as follows. A priestly teacher received special insight into God's will and calendar, clashed with leaders in Jerusalem over law and timing, and led a community into the wilderness. In turn, he was persecuted by a rival called the Wicked Priest, while a third figure, the Man of Lies, created internal trouble. Dates and identifications remain debated, but the pattern is not. Sectarian movements are born when timing, law, and leadership diverge beyond repair.

A brief word on two desert libraries

Because readers sometimes confuse the Dead Sea caves with another famous desert cache, a quick distinction is helpful. In 1945, near Nag Hammadi in Upper Egypt, peasants uncovered a jar of Coptic codices that preserve a different kind of library: Christian and Jewish mystical and philosophical texts, including collections of sayings attributed to Jesus. Those are late antique books written in Coptic, not Second Temple Hebrew scrolls, and they trace the fortunes of a different set of communities. The two discoveries share sand and secrecy, not authorship or theology.

Writing the Essenes with texture, not stereotype

Avoid calling them a desert cult or a monastic order without context. They were pious Jews attempting to live Scripture as law, poetry, and calendar all at once. They are severe by modern standards, yet their hymns are tender and their rules insist on truthfulness and care for the vulnerable. Their withdrawal was not escapism. It was a bid to become a living temple until the real one could be purified.

Reading like an Essene

Take one prophetic verse. Ask what it means for your community now. Identify a living teacher. Expect persecution. Hold a calendar that marks you as different. Pray and eat in order, and treat purity as preparation for hearing God.

Scribe of Qumran

SALFRAFICA

Essene Scribe of Qumran (1st c. BCE–1st c. CE)

Common myths you can safely retire

- *Myth:* The scrolls expose a conspiracy to hide Christianity's true origin.

Reality: they predate and parallel early Christianity. Their relevance is historical and comparative, not conspiratorial.

- *Myth:* Everything at Qumran was written on site.

  Reality: The library was mixed. Some texts were likely copied elsewhere and brought in. DNA and handwriting studies now help sort clusters without relying on guesswork.

- *Myth:* The Copper Scroll is a coded path to unfound gold that will one day solve everything.

  Reality: It is a unique text with a disputed purpose and no confirmed recoveries. Treat it as a historical artifact, not a treasure map.

Bringing it home

The Dead Sea Scrolls are not a curiosity. They are a set of voices, earnest and precise, that let you hear how a community took Scripture seriously enough to reframe its time, place, and meals around it. They walked out into the desert to live what they saw, copy what they believed, and wait for God to act. Whether you agree with their halakhah, you cannot miss their courage. Use them in your book to restore color to the Second Temple world, to make biblical law feel lived in, and to show how ideas incubate in communities long before they spark a movement.

If you stay in the caves and halls of Qumran long enough to smell the ink and the clay, you'll come away with a sense that the Bible is not a book that fell from the sky. It is a library made by people who argued, sang, copied, and kept time together. That is the secret the Essenes left in jars, and that is the hidden wisdom worth bringing back to light.

Chapter 6:

The Nag Hammadi Library – Gospels buried in the sands of Egypt

To comprehend why a jar of old books shook the study of Christian origins, begin with a picture that is anything but romantic: a peasant digging for fertilizer on a scrubby slope near the village of Nag Hammadi in Upper Egypt in 1945. He breaks open a tall clay jar, and out slide tightly bound papyrus codices written in Coptic, the last phase of the ancient Egyptian language. Within months, portions are in Cairo, one codex travels a shadowy route into Europe, and scholars realize that the cache preserves lost treatises and gospels once denounced and destroyed. The volume that wandered to Zurich becomes known as the Jung Codex, and it includes a text that early critics had mocked by name: a work called the Gospel of Truth. That single recovery proves two things at once: that the library was real, and that the heresiologists were sometimes describing actual titles rather than inventing slurs.

The codices are fourth-century copies of earlier compositions, many from the second century, and their physical features are as instructive as their theology. They are papyrus books, not scrolls, in a clear, unornamented hand, roughly twice as tall as wide, in Subachmimic Coptic, probably from around Assiut. One codex preserved has about a hundred pages; most originally had more. A dozen reached the Coptic Museum in Cairo, with another, the Jung Codex, separated early in the dispersal. The proximity of the find to early Pachomian monastic sites makes it plausible that monks hid them when certain writings became dangerous to possess.

What was actually in that jar

The cache was not a single book with a single voice; it was a small library. Among its best-known works are the Gospel of Thomas, a sayings collection attributed to the "Living Jesus," copied in Codex II; the Gospel of Truth, a rich homiletic meditation that many now place within the Valentinian circle; and treatises like the Apocryphon of John or the Tripartite Tractate. Thomas is the outlier that captured the world's attention, a series of 114 logia without narrative, miracle cycle, or passion story, a text that reads like a training manual for insight.

How to think about a sayings gospel: A sayings collection is not a biography. It is a curated set of voice-prints meant to be heard, recited, and lived. In Thomas, interpretation is part of salvation, because reading becomes a spiritual exercise.

Why were they buried?

The most economical explanation is also the most likely: controversy. By the late fourth century, bishops and imperial edicts were narrowing the scope of acceptable books. Monastic libraries held miscellaneous volumes, some deeply cherished by certain teachers. Hiding a chest, or a jar of codices, preserves them when public possession becomes risky. That is not a conspiracy narrative; it is a pattern we see elsewhere in late antique Egypt. While we cannot reconstruct every step between the scriptorium and the sand, the find context, the monastic geography, and the later polemics align too neatly to be accidental.

Sealing a Coptic Codex near
Nag Hammadi, c. 4th century CE

Reading the library: three windows into its world

1) The Gospel of Thomas, a handbook for the awake

Thomas does not offer apocalypse or prophecy; it offers a pedagogy of recognition. A short saying speaks to another, then undercuts it, then turns the reader inward. Its opening claim that those who live by the interpretation of these words will not "taste death" is a thesis about transformation through knowing. It gives no plot for devotion to follow; it gives practices of attention. The real subject is the human person who learns to see. That is why Thomas became the lightning rod: if salvation is a matter of inwardly awakened sight, who needs a single external arbiter of meaning?

The genius of Thomas lies in its refusal to decide for you. It puts parables beside aphorisms, riddles beside blunt instruction, and asks the student to cultivate an inner hearing. Read it as a laboratory notebook for consciousness, written in the idiom of the first centuries.

2) The Gospel of Truth, a sermon on joy that reads like a prayer

Unlike Thomas, the Gospel of Truth is not a sayings anthology; it is a flowing homily that starts with a thesis worthy of a cathedral inscription: the gospel means joy for those who know the Father. Ignorance produced terror and error, error shaped matter, and human beings fell into the sleep of forgetfulness. Christ appears as the fruit of knowing, hung upon the wood, tasted by those who become joyful and awake. The text enumerates emanations, wisdom, and word, and joy and love, but its heartbeat is not system building; it is the experience of being found by knowledge. Many scholars see this as a Valentinian text; some even propose composition by Valentinus in Rome around the mid-second century, before the more baroque systems flowered. That placement matters because it shows an early Christian writer, later deemed heretical, reading the New Testament intensively to speak of redemption and knowledge.

Notice the rhythm: knowledge is not trivia, it is wakefulness; the Son "in a similitude of flesh" is touchable and a guide; the goal is unity, not curiosity. That combination, mystical and scriptural, explains why the Gospel of Truth felt both familiar and strange when it reappeared.

3) Women in the circle, memory, and rivalry

Although the Gospel of Mary does not belong to the Nag Hammadi cache, it wove through the same streams of teaching, and it preserves voices that illuminate the world behind these codices. In that gospel, Mary reports a revelation dialogue from the Saviour, and her brothers debate whether to trust her. One disciple acknowledges that the Lord "loved" her more than the other women, and invites her to teach; later, another objects that the Lord would not speak to a woman secretly and prefers not to "turn and all listen to her." That tension tells you two things: that some circles prized a woman disciple as a chief interpreter of Jesus, and that anxiety about gendered authority provoked resistance. Read alongside Nag Hammadi works in which Mary asks searching questions or is named among key disciples, you see a spectrum, sometimes exemplary esteem, sometimes contested leadership. The library's landscape allowed for a woman who quotes scripture, recalls sayings, and is praised because her questions are precise and purposeful.

Mary's status, distilled: In multiple early dialogues, Mary speaks, interprets, and is affirmed as insightful; in some scenes a male disciple objects on gendered grounds. The friction itself is evidence that her voice mattered enough to provoke pushback.

Mary Magdalene Teaching: A Debate Over Whether to Listen

What unites these books

The library is diverse in genre, yet certain convictions recur.

1. **Knowing is salvific:** Ignorance is not a minor flaw; it is the root of fear and fragmentation. Knowledge is not mere information; it is recognition of origin and belonging that makes a person whole, which is why many of these texts press you to discover the inner place where the Father is known. In that frame, Jesus is revealer and physician, the one who wakes the sleeper.

2. **Scripture is a quarry:** These authors quote or allude to the apostolic writings constantly. That is one of the most inconvenient lessons of the Gospel of Truth. A so-called heretic in the mid-second century can be found using Matthew, John, Paul, Revelation, and more, not as ornaments, but as sources of grammar and hope. The Nag Hammadi books did not grow in a pagan field detached from the Jesus movement; they grew from within it, drawing on its texts even when they argued about their meaning.

3. **Christ is tangible and transformative:** Far from floating above the world, the revealer appears, teaches, is touched, and is said to attach the Father's disposition to the wood of the cross. The language can be mythic when it speaks of aeons, yet the soteriology is pastoral: bring the lost home, sober the drunk, console the terrified.

The artifact speaks: codices, copying, and circulation.

A book is a social machine. The Nag Hammadi codices show careful construction, papyrus folded into quires, sewn along the fold, and housed in leather covers. The copying is competent, with occasional hands visible. To an ancient reader, the choice of codex over scroll already signals a Christian milieu. The dialect points to Upper Egypt; the likely transmission route crosses monastic networks. The mixture of tractates within a single codex suggests small libraries built by accretion, not by a single editor. And then there is the economics: papyrus, leather, trained copyists, all of which imply sponsors who valued these works enough to invest in their making.

Why did the findings change the argument?

Before the library, most of what we knew of these currents came from their opponents. After the library, we could read them as they presented themselves. That single change re-weighted the conversation. A homily like the Gospel of Truth complicates the caricature that all "Gnostics" were anti-Christian philosophers; it reads like a sermon soaked in scripture. At the same time, the library does preserve the speculative habits that defined certain schools, with lists of emanations and mythic etiologies of ignorance. The point is not to romanticize or to demonize, it is to listen.

Case studies that make the material concrete

Thomas as practice

Take three adjacent sayings and work them like exercises. One pushes you to seek; another tells you that finding will trouble you; a third urges you to become one. That sequence is not a riddle for its own sake; it is a training in expectation and perseverance. Read aloud, repeat, and watch how the mind orbits back to its center. The ancient compiler trusted that repeated hearing would till the soil of attention. That is why Thomas has been compared to other wisdom traditions; it shares a pedagogy, not a doctrine.

Truth as proclamation

If you stand in a small church and hear the Gospel of Truth read aloud, the theme that rings is joy through knowing. The treatise sketches a fall into oblivion, then dwells on the revealer who leads the lost out, like daylight ending a bad dream. It lists attributes in chains, wisdom, word, intelligence, joy, glory, love, faith, not as an abstract catalogue, but as a rising chorus. It is less concerned with forgiveness than with recognition, less with law than with the sudden relief of waking. The text's Christ opens the book of the living and then teaches as a master in a school, with little ones as the ideal hearers.

Mary as interpreter

When Mary speaks, she does not claim domination; she recalls words and offers meaning. In one striking scene, she turns grieving disciples inward to the Good One, then narrates her encounter with the Saviour. The debate that follows is telling: first an invitation to share, then a denial rooted in gender, then a reconciliation by another disciple urging peace. That arc, recognition, resistance, reconciliation, feels painfully human. It documents a community learning how to hear from a voice that some had not expected to lead.

The human stakes

The most tired debate about this book is whether it is dangerous or liberating. The more fruitful question is, what kind of person do these texts try to form? In Thomas, a person who has learned to recognize the inner source and to become "single." In Truth, a person who lives in joy because forgetfulness has been healed. In the dialogues with Mary, a person who trusts that the Spirit speaks where the community did not always expect. In practical terms, this book trains attention, memory, and the courage to receive.

That is why it continues to matter. It does not replace the canonical gospels, and doesn't fit comfortably under someone else's orthodoxy either. It is a witness to a world where Christians argued ferociously about what salvation is and how it happens, and where books were precious enough to hide in jars when the argument turned dangerous.

A single sentence to carry forward: These buried gospels insist that waking to knowledge is a form of joy, and that the revealer's work is to make that joy durable in a frightened world.

Appendix for the curious reader

A note on discovery and publication: The Jung Codex, separated early, was photographed, transcribed, and translated into French and then English. Scholars debated the title Gospel of Truth that Irenaeus had scorned; the internal evidence made the identification compelling. The codex's Coptic shows a likely fourth-century copy date; its conceptual roots reach back to the mid-second century. Across the broader cache, codicology, dialect, and intertextuality anchor the books in Upper Egypt, with the Pachomian landscape as a plausible setting for burial.

A note on Thomas and its impact: Thomas' discovery in Codex II was not just a media event; it redrew the map of sources for Jesus traditions. Whether one reads it as an independent sayings tradition or as a collage, the text forced scholars to reckon with a Jesus remembered as a teacher of recognition rather than an apocalyptic herald. Its framing of gnosis, not as elitist code but as consciousness, shaped the modern reception.

Rediscovering the Gospels: 1896-1959

1896	1945	1956	1959

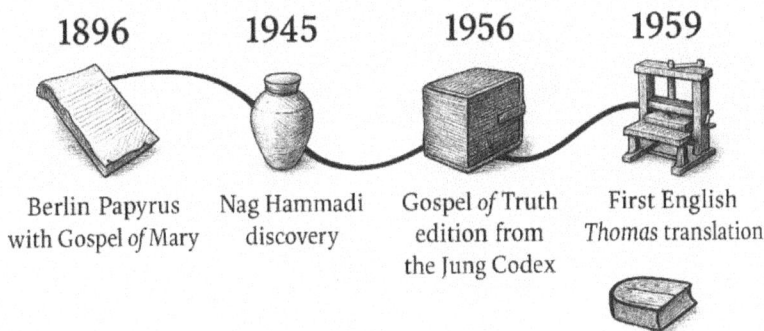

| Berlin Papyrus with Gospel *of* Mary | Nag Hammadi discovery | Gospel *of* Truth edition from the Jung Codex | First English *Thomas* translation |

To read this work well, resist two temptations. First, do not flatten them into one ideology. Second, do not treat them as exotic curios. Read them as voices of Christians who loved scripture, who believed Christ heals forgetfulness by giving knowledge, and who trusted that the kingdom is within and among us. That is the secret the sands of Egypt kept for fifteen hundred years.

Chapter 7:

The Lost Jewish Texts – Jubilees, Solomon, and apocryphal psalms

If you want to see how living, contested, and frankly electrifying Second Temple Judaism really was, do not start with what everybody already knows. Step off the main road. Sit with the books that did not make it into most Bibles, the texts copied, cherished, and sometimes hidden by communities who believed they were guarding the real schedule of heaven, the true shape of Israel's hope, and the dangerous names that move unseen powers. Three clusters show the terrain with unusual clarity: the Book of Jubilees, the Solomonic traditions, and the apocryphal psalms. Read together, they expose a world where calendars were weapons, hymns were manifestos, and a king's wisdom could command angels and bind demons.

Jubilees: the calendar of heaven, the story retold

What it is

Jubilees is a Second Temple era retelling of Genesis and early Exodus, presented as a revelation given to Moses by an angel on Sinai. Its author is not improvising for style. He is rearranging time itself. History is divided into fifty-year "jubilees" and seven-year "weeks," a grid that turns the biblical past into a meticulously dated timeline. Festivals, covenants, and even the cycles of agricultural life are slotted into this master schedule. The book insists the proper year has 364 days, four exact quarters of 13 weeks each, which keeps Sabbaths and feasts from "drifting." This is not a minor arithmetic choice. It is a theological marker: the heavens run on order, not on the wobble of the moon. Communities that adopted this calendar saw themselves as aligning with the angels and correcting a nation that had forgotten the right time.

Jubilees does more than timekeeping. It rewrites the patriarchal narratives with halakhic clarity. Dietary rules appear earlier, intermarriage boundaries harden, the priestly line is traced with care, and figures like Noah and Abraham are cast as ideal observant prototypes. An adversarial figure, Mastema, stalks the narrative, a way of explaining moral evil and testing without collapsing everything into fatalism. The point is pastoral as much as polemical: Israel's story was always meant to be read as law woven into time.

Where it was loved and why that matters

We know the book circulated widely in the late Second Temple period. Fragments of Jubilees in Hebrew turned up among the Dead Sea Scrolls, a strong sign that sectarian groups, likely Qumran circles, valued it. And one ancient church still reads it as Scripture today, because the Ethiopian Orthodox Tewahedo canon preserves Jubilees as a holy book. That combination, cave fragments in Hebrew and a living canonical status, makes Jubilees a rare window into both early Jewish practice and long continuity in Christian Ethiopia.

Why the calendar fights mattered

The calendar is a community. If your Passover falls on a different day, your loyalty is different, too. A fixed 364-day year means Sabbath never wanders, festivals land on the same weekday every year, and the temple schedule runs like clockwork. To adherents, that proved fidelity to creation's architecture. To critics, it looked like sectarian stubbornness.

The dispute shows how practical details, like counting days, become markers of identity when empires loom and authority is contested.

The 364-day 'complete year'

Jubilees' year equals 52 weeks, four seasons of 13 weeks. Festivals recur on fixed weekdays, which the book treats as proof of cosmic order. The Dead Sea Scrolls preserve this system in multiple texts, showing it was not an isolated idea but part of a broad calendar tradition.

Solomon beyond Kings: wisdom, hymns, and the lore of names

The biblical Solomon is a builder, judge, and proverb-maker. Second Temple and later writers took that seed and grew a forest. Not everything wearing Solomon's name is the same species, so let us sort the grove. Each work tells you something different about the hopes and fears of its readers.

Wisdom of Solomon: Jewish Alexandria speaks philosophy in Scripture's accent

Composed in Greek by a Jewish author in Alexandria, usually dated to the first century BCE, Wisdom presents Sophia, Wisdom personified, as the breath and radiance of God. It defends Israel's faith using the tools of Hellenistic rhetoric and speaks of immortality with arresting calm. Later Christian theology would mine its language to speak about the Word and the Spirit, but its roots are Jewish, urbane, and confident. Read it to hear a diaspora voice refusing to choose between Athens and Jerusalem.

Jewish Scholar Reading a Scroll, Roman Alexandria
(1st-2nd century CE)

Psalms of Solomon: after Pompey, aching for a clean king

Eighteen psalms, probably in Hebrew originally, survive in Greek and Syriac. The collection breathes the air of the 60s to 40s BCE. Rome's general Pompey enters Jerusalem, desecration follows, and the city reels. Out of that shock comes a fierce hope for a Davidic messiah who will purge injustice and shepherd the faithful. This is not vague spirituality. It is a theological reading of current events, asking for a ruler who loves mercy and hates corruption, who expels the lawless and heals the penitent. The result became one of the clearest Second Temple portraits of a coming Davidic king.

JERUSALEM, 63 BCE –
Roman Standards Near the Temple Gate

Odes of Solomon: baptismal joy from a Jewish Christian singer

Forty-two odes, preserved primarily in Syriac, were likely composed in the late first or early second century CE. They sound like early Christian hymns, but you will hear Jewish textures throughout, and resonances with Qumran phrases and the Gospel of John. Themes of new birth, living water, and Spirit-filled praise flow through them. Think of a mikveh overflowing into a baptismal pool. If you want to feel how Jewish devotion turned naturally into Christian worship language, the Odes are a perfect bridge.

Living Water: Early Christian Baptism (1st–2nd Century)

Testament of Solomon: a handbook of power framed as a king's memoir

Here Solomon receives a heaven-given ring and compels demons to work on the Temple, interrogating each spirit by name, function, and countermeasure. The work, in Greek with complex transmission, likely took shape in late antiquity, drawing on older Jewish traditions and expanding with Christian layers. It is not a temple liturgy and not a synagogue sermon. It reads like learned folklore turned into a spiritual manual, where the names of angels, planetary forces, and secret prayers meet the idea that wise rule includes mastery over chaos. Its popularity in later magical literature shows how persistent that idea became.

Solomon's reputation across time

In Jewish Scripture, Solomon is sage and builder. In Hellenistic Judaism, he becomes a voice for reasoned piety. In later Jewish and Christian lore, he is also the king who knows the names. That shift does not erase Scripture's portrait, it shows how communities used his figure to think about power, healing, and the right use of secret knowledge.

Testament of Solomon

Michael
Gabriel
Raphael
Uriel
Anael
Zadkiel
Cassiel

Bound demon

Signet ring

Signet ring

King Solomon and the Bound Spirit (after the *Testament of Solomon*)

The apocryphal psalms: Davidic music beyond the Masoretic 150

Open the standard Hebrew Psalter and you will find 150 psalms. At Qumran, the picture is more fluid. The large Psalms Scroll known as 11QPs-a arranges familiar psalms in a different order, inserts extra compositions, and ends with a prose colophon claiming that David wrote thousands of songs, including 364 to be used for daily offerings, plus special sets for Sabbaths and festivals. That is a liturgical vision, not trivia. It imagines Israel's worship saturating every day with song.

Psalm 151: the psalm that tells its own origin story

Most Western readers first meet Psalm 151 in the Greek Septuagint. It is short and autobiographical, David telling how he was chosen and how he killed Goliath. For a long time, scholars thought the psalm was a Greek-era addition. The Dead Sea Scrolls changed that picture by preserving two related Hebrew compositions that together underlie the Greek form. In other words, an ancient Hebrew idea flowed into Greek, and both streams survive. That is canon formation in real time.

Psalms 154 and 155: wisdom and repentance from the fringes of the canon

These psalms lived in Syriac Bibles and, surprisingly, in the Qumran Psalms Scroll in Hebrew. Psalm 154 reads like a communal wisdom exhortation, calling the people to unite around the fear of the Lord and the personified Lady Wisdom. Psalm 155 is a repentant plea that echoes Psalms 22 and 51, right at home in liturgy. Their presence shows that circles around the Dead Sea curated a wider hymnbook than the later fixed Jewish canon, borrowing and refining as they prayed.

What makes a psalm "in" or "out"

Canon is not a purity test for truth. It is a boundary for shared reading. Qumran's willingness to sing beyond 150 shows that ordinary worshippers felt free to use new and old poems that matched their theology. Later rabbinic tradition standardized the Psalter. The impulse behind both moves is pastoral, not conspiratorial: communities need a common book to chant together. The surprise is how long that process stayed open.

What these texts reveal beneath the surface

A moving canon, not a broken faith

The canon was not born fixed. Communities tried, adopted, and sometimes set aside texts for centuries. Jubilees and the apocryphal psalms show the testing ground. The Ethiopian canon's embrace of Jubilees proves the story did not end the same way everywhere. That is not chaos. That is the ordinary life of a tradition with global branches.

Competing authorities, competing calendars

When Jubilees pushes a 364-day year, it is pushing more than math. It is a claim that right worship depends on right time, that Israel's leaders lost the plot, and that a remnant has held the line. Qumran's calendar texts say the same. You can feel the tension between the temple establishment and the reformist sect. In our terms, it is a scheduling fight with metaphysical stakes.

Messianic hope with sharp edges

The Psalms of Solomon do not daydream about a generic savior. They name injustice, remember Rome's violence, and pray for a son of David who purifies the city. That tone helps explain why messianic expectations at the turn of the era were so charged. The prayers are not about personal uplift. They are about public righteousness under God's chosen king.

Wisdom that speaks multiple languages

The Wisdom of Solomon shows Jewish theology speaking fluent Greek without losing itself. Odes of Solomon show Jewish imagery, water and spirit, and temple, blooming into Christian song. Both prove that Second Temple faith could be loyal to Torah and hospitable to new intellectual climates.

Power and prudence

The Testament of Solomon fascinates because it touches a nerve: the desire for holy power to set the world right. Catalogs of demons and angels, ring and seal, exorcisms by name, all show a world where prayer and technique mingle. The healthy instinct here is that disorder needs wise authority. The danger is to confuse curiosity with discipleship. Traditions that kept this material tended to pair it with moral discipline, not spectacle.

How to use these texts without getting lost

Read them like maps, not idols. Jubilees maps time. Odes map devotion. The apocryphal psalms map the lived range of prayer. Psalms of Solomon map political hope. Wisdom maps Jewish thought in diaspora. Testament of Solomon maps the folklore of power. They are guides to worlds that produced both Jesus' earliest followers and rabbinic sages.

Cross-read with the known canon. When Jubilees advances law into the patriarchs' lives, ask how that reframing highlights or critiques the Torah. When the Psalms of Solomon imagine a purifying king, read them next to Isaiah's servant and Zechariah's humble ruler. When Odes sing of living water, hold them beside John 4 and the mikveh practices of the time.

Respect transmission. Qumran's hymnbook was not the same as the later Masoretic Psalter. The Ethiopian canon is not the same as the Protestant table of contents. These differences are not failures. They are the documentary record of a faith that spread across languages, continents, and centuries.

Questions people always ask, answered fast.

Is Jubilees trying to replace the Torah?

No. It is trying to interpret it, to argue that the law is older and more cosmic than some thought, and to anchor that claim in a calendar that reflects creation's symmetry. The insistence on 364 days is the vehicle for a larger point about order and fidelity.

Are the apocryphal psalms "less inspired" because they are not in the Masoretic 150?

In ancient practice, inspiration and canonicity were related but not identical. Communities prayed with texts that matched their convictions, then later generations standardized for unity. The Dead Sea Scrolls show that process in motion, not the absence of inspiration.

Did Jews really expect a warrior messiah?

Some did, some did not, but the Psalms of Solomon prove that a strong Davidic, purifying hope was real for many after Roman intrusion. That stream fed later messianic debates.

Is the Testament of Solomon "magic" or theology?

It borrows the machinery of late antique ritual power while assuming a monotheistic frame in which God's authority, often mediated by angelic names, is ultimate. Its enduring appeal is precisely at that border of folklore and faith.

A final orientation, text by text

Jubilees gives you the grid that orders all things. If you grasp that grid, you understand why some Jews were ready to break with mainstream calendars rather than betray creation's pattern. It also explains why their sabbaths, feasts, and moral boundaries were non-negotiable.

The Wisdom of Solomon lets you hear a Jewish mind address a Greek city with poise. It is a gift to modern readers who juggle faith and pluralism.

Psalms of Solomon pull your prayer out of abstraction and back into streets, trials, and governance. They keep messianic longing honest because they remember conquest and compromise by name.

Odes of Solomon sing the moment when Jewish symbols saturate Christian worship. If you want to feel how the earliest Christians thought, not just what they argued, the Odes are a treasure.

The Testament of Solomon is your test case in discernment. It reveals the magnetism of sacred technique and the perennial human wish for control. Handle it as folklore orbiting theology, not as a manual.

Apocryphal Psalms show the Psalter as a living book before it was a closed book. If you want people to sing, you sometimes need more songs. Qumran obliged.

Part III — Power, Control, and Suppression

Chapter 8: The Vatican's Secret Archives – Locked doors and hidden truths

You do not have to believe in a conspiracy to know that control over memory is control over meaning. The institution that has guarded more of Christianity's memory than any other is the Vatican, and for centuries, its records sat behind keys few could touch. Today, scholars can apply for access, yet the instincts of custody, gatekeeping, and narrative management did not disappear with a change of name from the Vatican Secret Archives to the Vatican Apostolic Archive. They persist in practices, in protocols, and in how the past is framed. This chapter opens those doors conceptually, and it ties what we can learn from the Church's own cupboards to the currents of early Christian writing that survived outside them, including texts that present different portraits of Jesus and his first followers.

What the Archive is, and what it is not

The Archive is not a single dark vault; it is a sprawling administrative memory of a global monarchy and spiritual center. Think of it as layered strata.

1. **Curial records:** correspondence, decrees, and case files that show how doctrine and discipline were managed.

2. **Diplomatic series:** letters and reports between Rome and courts or colonies from Europe to Africa and Asia.

3. **Judicial dossiers:** from the Holy Office, from marriage tribunals, from processes that weighed orthodoxy, pastoral practice, or political loyalty.

4. **Financial and property ledgers**: the mundane backbone of power.

This mass of paper shows the Church arguing with itself, with kingdoms, and with movements that carried the Bible into streets, workshops, and classrooms. It also reveals what administrators feared, what they protected, and what they preferred to forget. The Archive is less a museum of scandals and more a record of management, yet that management often decided which ideas were preserved, which were sidelined, and which were buried under the label of error.

Why "secrecy" mattered

For most of history, secrecy was not about hiding shame; it was about protecting jurisdiction. In a world of rival crowns and bishops, documents were ammunition. A sealed register could be the difference between a monastery keeping its lands or a nascent nation breaking a concordat. Over time, that habit of custody hardened into a culture. When you are the steward of the keys, you develop an instinct for which doors stay shut.

Access has loosened, but the Archive still teaches a critical lesson: the story of Christianity was curated. Curation does not mean fabrication; it means selection. The "canon" was a selection, theological curricula were selections, and the administrative record preserves those selections better than it preserves the alternatives.

The alternatives, and why they mattered

Outside the official pathways, we possess texts that tell the Jesus story differently, or that amplify voices the canonical gospels mention only briefly. One striking example bears the name of a woman. In a Coptic gospel attributed to Mary, the storyline shows her receiving teaching and recognition, then facing pushback from male disciples who question whether Jesus would have spoken privately to her. The episode crystallizes a contest over authority inside the earliest circles of believers, and it reveals why later gatekeepers preferred clearer chains of office.

A different text, often called the Gospel of Truth, reads like a theological homily. It speaks of ignorance, fear, and the joy that comes when knowledge of the Father unties those bonds. It is associated with a sophisticated school of thought in the second century, and it was preserved among the writings unearthed near Nag Hammadi in Upper Egypt in 1945. That desert find included codices copied in Coptic, one of which, long kept apart and nicknamed for the institute that received it, preserved this "Gospel of Truth." The work's themes revolve around ignorance giving birth to error and the need for a revealing knowledge, a vocabulary that tells you why administrators with a taste for uniform catechisms viewed it with suspicion.

Then there is a sayings collection whose first appearance in modern times was also in those jars near Nag Hammadi. It contains 114 short logia attributed to "the living Jesus," with almost no narrative frame. It reads like a handbook for interior work, not a passion story, and it gives readers the sense that the task is transformation through understanding rather than adherence to a story arc. Anyone comparing that lean, aphoristic approach with the procedural tone of administrative Christianity will understand why each tradition valued different kinds of writing.

These texts do not sit on a shelf in Rome's administrative memory because they were not the paperwork of Rome's government. They do, however, reveal the theological and social possibilities available in the first centuries, and they help us read the Archive's silence. Where you find thick files on bishops correcting "disorders," it is reasonable to infer that creative forms of teaching or leadership stood behind those corrections, even if the alternative voices come to us from Egypt's sands rather than from a Roman registry.

What "locked doors" look like in practice

A locked door can be literal, a fond restriction for conservation, or because of diplomatic sensitivities. More often, it is methodological.

- **Cataloging that deters:** series titles are technical, inventories are partial, and finding aids sometimes assume you already know what you are looking for.

- **Permissions that shape questions:** scholars request items by shelfmark, so a researcher working on women's teaching, for example, is funneled toward male-authored synodal acts, not toward forgotten convent files that might preserve counterexamples.

- **Time pressure:** permission windows, daily page limits, and restricted photography nudge you to confirm what you came to prove, not to wander.

None of this is a villain's plot. It is how archives maintain order, yet it tends to favor established narratives. If you already believe leadership descended neatly from apostolic men to bishops, the Archive gives you mountains of supportive evidence, because that is who was writing and filing.

Hidden truths, and the kind of truth the Archive can and cannot give

There are two kinds of hidden truth in this context.

1. **Unknown because uncataloged or inaccessible:** files that few have examined, series that were long closed, material that only now becomes legible as cataloging improves.

2. **Unknown because never written down or deliberately left out:** the voices of lay women and men who debated, taught, prayed, and organized, yet left fewer official traces.

The first kind yields to patient work. The second kind requires triangulation with sources that survived outside official custody. Those desert books help. In a text bearing Mary's name, you see a woman explaining visions and teaching discouraged male disciples, with one of them asking why she should be believed. That scene demonstrates that early Christian communities wrestled with who could speak authoritatively, and it suggests that the narrowing of voices was a process, not an assumption from the start.

Likewise, a homily like the Gospel of Truth shows a style of reflection that feels less like a legal code and more like a spiritual therapy. It talks about ignorance shaping a world of fear, then joy coming through knowledge that reorients the self, imagery that sits uneasily with administrative definitions and penalties. When orthodoxy hardened, such literature became suspect, not always because it denied Christ, but because it distributed authority differently, privileging interior grasp over external warrants.

How suppression worked without burning every book

People imagine a bonfire. Often it was subtler. Control depended on five levers.

- **Curriculum:** what future clergy read shaped what they could imagine.

- **Licensing:** printers, professors, and preachers needed approvals.

- **Pastoral tone:** the faithful were taught that certain ideas were spiritually dangerous, which dried up copyists and audiences.

- **Discipline:** troublemakers lost pulpits, not always their lives.

- **Record keeping:** once an opinion was classified as an error, future cases cited the file, and the category stiffened over time.

When alternative gospels survive, they do so because they were copied in communities beyond Roman control, or because they were buried rather than destroyed, which is precisely what happened with several codices discovered in 1945.

The Archive as a mirror: what it reveals about power

Reading the Archive beside the early literature that did not pass through its filing rooms teaches a simple thing about power. Institutions reward voices that stabilize the institution. That is not a unique flaw of Rome; it is how all durable bureaucracies work. What matters for our purposes is recognizing the cost, so that in the present we can read across the grain.

- When you see synods legislating women's roles in sharp terms, remember that other communities, attested in early texts, still imagined women teaching, interpreting, and leading prayer. The resistance to such roles appears on both sides of the divide, inside official minutes and inside narratives where a male disciple challenges a woman's authority.

- When you see decrees demanding doctrinal clarity, set next to them the literature that values transformative understanding as the heart of salvation. The contrast shows why administrative religion and interiorist writings often clashed, even when both affirmed Christ.

Myths worth correcting

Let us clear a few common mistakes so we can focus on the real issues.

- **Myth:** The Archive hides proof that the Christian canon was invented late in a smoke-filled room.

  Reality: the canon emerged over time through reading, worship, and argument. The Archive preserves parts of that process, but the most revealing evidence for alternative paths often sits outside it, in texts that never entered Roman custody. The existence of those texts is not proof of a hidden canon; it is proof of diversity that selection has narrowed.

- **Myth:** There is a single "forbidden gospel" that would overturn everything.

  Reality: the surviving non-canonical literature offers a mosaic, not a silver bullet. A gospel attributed to Mary shows contested authority and women's leadership, a homily called the Gospel of Truth articulates salvation as knowledge that dispels fear, and a sayings collection associated with Thomas models an interior pedagogy. Each illuminates, none replaces the whole.

- **Myth:** secrecy always means guilt.

Reality: secrecy usually means habit and jurisdiction. The problem is not secrecy as such; it is the way secrecy, routine, and power shape the record of memory.

Title: What the "Secret" really hides

- Secrecy in Rome's Archive is mostly about control of jurisdiction and narrative, not about a single hidden bombshell.
- The most challenging early Christian alternatives survive outside Rome's filing system, and they show a wider range of authority and spiritual method than the official story suggests.
- Reading the Archive and the desert books together gives a truer picture of how the faith narrowed into a stable public form.

The human stakes behind the papers

Files can make us forget flesh and blood. The texts outside Rome's custody put people back into view. In one narrative, a woman disciple is praised for insight, then scolded for speaking too much, exactly the kind of social tension any movement faces when charisma meets hierarchy. In another, salvation is presented as a process of waking from fear through knowledge of God, which sounds less like a police report and more like a changed life. In the sayings, we hear the voice of a teacher who expects students to grow spiritually, not merely to memorize answers. These are not enemies of faith; they are different grammars of faith, and the Archive's story is, in part, the story of which grammar became official.

What the Archive still owes the world

The Church has done more in the last century to open its cupboards than in the previous four combined. Even so, three debts remain.

1. **Better guides:** make finding aids that do not require insider knowledge.

2. **Proactive disclosure:** release curated digital sets on topics the public rightly cares about, not only the ones scholars already know.

3. **Contextual honesty:** when presenting the canonical story, acknowledge, without fear, the early diversity that the institution did not adopt.

A Church confident in truth should be a Church confident in memory. Memory that includes only the winners is propaganda. Memory that includes the friction is history, and history tends to strengthen communities in the long run.

How does this change the way we tell the story of the Bible

The canon is not a scandal; it is a decision tree. The Archive preserves the forks that were chosen. The desert books preserve branches that were pruned. A serious history does not reattach every branch, and it does not slash the trunk; it sketches the whole tree so readers see how a living faith grew into a public religion.

- A gospel named for a woman reminds us that women held spiritual authority in some early communities, and that male resistance to that authority is almost as old as the movement itself. That knowledge does not cancel the canon; it rounds out the memory.

- A homiletic "gospel" centered on knowledge as healing reframes the purpose of doctrine as therapy for fear. That insight does not abolish creeds; it challenges us to use creeds as medicine, not as weapons.

- A sayings collection with no narrative asks believers to grow by interpretation, not only by repetition. That method can enrich catechesis even within a canonical church.

A final walk down the corridor

Picture a researcher leaving the Vatican reading room at dusk, fingers ink-stained, a notebook full of shelfmarks and questions. Across an ocean of time, a jar in a desert once broke open, and different kinds of "good news" spilled into the light. Put those two images together, and you get the real secret. The archive is not so much hiding a single truth as it is preserving the choices that made one kind of Christianity public and powerful. The hidden truths are in the margins, in the habits, and in the alternatives that had to find other custodians.

If we are willing to read the official files with the same patience we bring to the alternative gospels, we can have a history that is both faithful and free. Faithful to the fact that a church did govern, teach, and preserve. Free to admit that the movement began with more voices than the ones that signed the decrees, including a woman who taught, a preacher who spoke of fear giving way to knowledge, and a teacher whose sayings still unsettle us into growth.

Chapter 9:

Banned Bibles and Burned Translations – Why ordinary believers were kept in the dark

They say a church is built on rock, yet for long stretches of history, its foundation was paper, ink, and the strict control of both. If you want to understand how ordinary believers were kept away from the words that shaped their souls, follow the trail of manuscripts chained to lecterns, translation licenses, secret readings at night, and the smoke of bonfires where books crackled like kindling. This is a story about language and power, about who gets to say what God said, and about how gatekeepers turned the people of the book into people who had to ask for the key.

The simplest mechanism of control: language, literacy, and the pulpit bottleneck

For centuries, access to scripture depended on clergy who could read and interpret for a largely illiterate population. Latin functioned as both a bridge and a barrier. In cathedral schools, Latin opened archives and commentaries. In village life, it separated the altar from the nave. When a priest read, the congregation heard selected passages wrapped in homily, then walked home with a memory shaped by that mediation.

That arrangement did not begin as a conspiracy. It began as a necessity. Books were rare, ink was dear, and copying a Bible took a scribe months. But necessity easily becomes policy. Once leaders saw that control of language meant control of meaning, the rule hardened: vernacular readings were risky, private copies without approval were suspect, and unsupervised interpretation could be branded as error.

Medieval Nave

The Chained Bible"

From disagreement to destruction: when argument turned into ash

From the start, Christian communities argued about which writings carried weight and which did not. Disputes were expected in a growing movement spread across languages, cultures, and trade routes. What made the difference in the long run was not only which books were persuasive, but which books survived when priests, bishops, or magistrates decided that certain pages were too dangerous to circulate.

Scribes copied what communities valued. Then, officials seized what communities were not supposed to value. Fire became a policy tool. A banned book erased with a sponge or burned in a square does more than disappear. It broadcasts a warning to anyone holding a similar copy under the bed.

Why leaders feared a free Bible

Look at the reasons leaders gave when they explained bans and burnings. They were not shy about the rationale.

1. **Doctrinal drift:** If anyone can translate a verse, anyone can bend it. Leaders feared rival readings that would erode cohesion. The fear was not abstract. Every century produced movements that quoted scripture against the established line, from apocalyptic date setters to antinomian sects.

2. **Social order:** Scripture is full of radical claims, including reversals of power and wealth. Officials worried that blunt vernacular readings, announced in a market square, could inflame unrest. They saw translation as more than a linguistic act. It was a transfer of moral authority from pulpit to street.

3. **Institutional survival:** Priestly training created a class invested with professional interpretation. A lay Bible in every home would dilute that role. Gatekeeping protected position, revenue, and the system that trained successors.

None of those motives alone explains the whole picture. Together, they describe a durable strategy: keep the text scarce, keep it technical, and punish unsanctioned attempts to change either condition.

The rise of alternatives: when other gospels complicated the story

Control is easiest when there is one canon, one text, one language. Real history was messier. Besides the familiar four gospels, ancient

Christians preserved sayings collections, wisdom sermons, and dialogues attributed to Jesus and his earliest followers. Their existence alone shows that the landscape of early Christianity was wide, not narrow, and that many communities circulated Jesus traditions that did not fit later expectations.

One such work, commonly called the Gospel of Truth and associated with a stream of thought linked to a teacher named Valentinus, survived in a fourth-century Coptic codex discovered near Nag Hammadi in Upper Egypt in 1945. The find was accidental, the result of peasants unearthing a jar of codices in the desert. The text presents salvation as knowledge of the Father revealed in Jesus, and it reads like a meditation rather than a narrative, which clashed with later preferences for tight doctrinal summaries and public creeds.

Another collection, the Gospel of Thomas, preserves 114 sayings attributed to Jesus, without a birth story, miracle tales, or passion narrative. It appears in the same cache of codices, the Nag Hammadi library, and emphasizes awakening through interpretation and practice. It is terse, sometimes riddling, and it puts responsibility back onto the listener: live the interpretation instead of waiting for an external authority to deliver it. Such a tone, direct and interior, made later leaders wary about what might happen if ordinary people took those sayings to heart without supervision.

There is also a text titled the Gospel of Mary, remarkable because it centers a woman disciple as a bearer of teaching and a stabilizing voice among male followers who doubt her. In that work, Mary speaks as a student who received instruction and as a leader who calms conflict, while some male disciples question her status. The very idea that a gospel could circulate under a woman's name and that she could be presented as particularly loved by the Lord unsettled later readers who preferred a tighter line on who could teach. The debates around that text display both admiration for Mary's insight and anxiety about her authority.

Why these alternative writings mattered

These texts do not need to replace the canon to matter. They matter because their survival shows that early believers copied, read, and argued over a wider range of Jesus traditions than a later uniform story suggests. Their themes, interior knowledge, contested leadership, and different literary forms highlight why gatekeepers later treated certain books as threats worth suppressing.

Nag Hammadi–Style Coptic Codex, Jar Shards

The medieval lockdown: rules that fenced the text

As Christianity moved from a persecuted minority to imperial ally and then to cultural default in Western Europe, the church refined control into procedure. The logic was simple. If unlicensed text creates unlicensed meaning, then regulate each link in the chain.

Copying moved into scriptoria with rules on exemplars. Preaching followed lectionary calendars, so the laity heard selected readings tied to the liturgical year. Parish Bibles were literally chained to desks to prevent theft, which also prevented private reading. Local synods and councils issued decrees limiting lay possession of certain texts, especially when movements rose that quoted scripture against the hierarchy. If a passage could be claimed by dissidents, access was tightened.

Then came the printing press, and with it the panic. The same technology that outfitted church libraries with cheap breviaries gave every determined reader a chance to own a Bible and compare the official translation with the words of a neighbor who had tried a different rendering. The response was swift: licensing for printers, privileges for official editions, and bans on unapproved translations. It was no longer enough to control the pulpit. Authorities tried to control the workshop and the warehouse.

CUM PRIVILEGIO:
An Early Print Shop, c. 15000

Translators under suspicion: when names became warnings

Translators were the hinge between a distant text and the language of the street. When that hinge swung without permission, it squeaked. Many were harried, imprisoned, exiled, or executed. Some were condemned long after their deaths, their bones exhumed and burned in symbolic acts meant to warn the living. Others worked under patronage and protection, but even patrons could not always shield a translator who pushed beyond approved phrasing.

The pattern is clear across borders and centuries. A translator chooses idiom over gloss, sense over letter, and is accused of smuggling doctrine under the cover of vocabulary. A bishop hears that households are reading aloud after supper and opens proceedings against the owner who distributed copies. Book smugglers hide quires in barrels, and port inspectors learn to sift for paper. It is an unromantic cat-and-mouse story, yet the stakes remained spiritual and social at once.

Why alternative gospels terrified gatekeepers more than rival preachers

A rival preacher can be silenced if needed. A rival book is a factory for rival preachers. That is why authorities who had learned to tolerate local preachers with eccentric emphases often treated certain books as intolerable. A book multiplies, travels, and endures. It creates communities of interpretation that share phrases and metaphors. It seeds a memory that persists even if the original copy is destroyed. That durability made the alternative Jesus traditions, like those found at Nag Hammadi, especially threatening in principle, even if only a few scholars ever saw them for centuries.

Consider how a text like the Gospel of Thomas functions. It invites us to find meaning through a direct encounter with a saying rather than through a priest's chain of authorities. A leader who wants to keep interpretation within a supervised ladder of commentary will see such a text as bypass surgery on the entire system. That is not paranoia. It is a correct assessment of the genre.

Or take the Gospel of Mary and its portrayal of a woman disciple who receives and transmits instruction. That storyline poses a challenge to any later policy that restricts who may teach or preach, and it explains why later readers, eager to tidy the past, expressed discomfort with scenes that centered her leadership. The text preserves both affirmation and resistance inside the same narrative, a mirror of the historical tension it reflects.

How suppression worked in practice

Confiscate stock from an unlicensed printer.
Interrogate sellers for supplier names.
Pressure patrons who funded a translation team.
Prohibit unapproved public readings in marketplaces and homes.
Make examples through public burnings of books and, in the harshest cases, people.
The method combined legal teeth, property control, and reputational fear. It did not require a large police force, just consistent penalties and the cooperation of local officials

The cost to ordinary believers: what people lost when the Bible was locked away

People did not only lose pages. They lost skills and habits that come with regular, unsupervised reading.

They lost the practice of comparing translations, which trains discernment and vocabulary. They lost household liturgies that grow when families read together and apply stories to daily life. They lost the confidence that comes from grappling with difficult passages without waiting for permission to think aloud.

They also lost voices that would have broadened their imagination. Alternative texts would not have solved all problems, and some contain ideas that later readers will reject for good reasons. Yet the mere presence of a sayings collection like Thomas or a revelatory dialogue like Mary increases the interpretive range of a Christian imagination. It invites ethical reflection through multiple lenses rather than a single official angle.

How suppression reshaped teaching, preaching, and memory

When you narrow the text, you narrow preaching. When you narrow preaching, you narrow memory. Over time, communities forget that alternatives ever existed. The church calendar keeps its rhythm, but the range of stories and themes that can be raised in a sermon shrinks to what is printed and approved. This concentrates power in commentaries and catechisms. It elevates the status of professional interpreters while lowering the expectations of lay insight.

That effect lingers even after the bans are lifted. People trained to hear only one voice at a lectern may hesitate to speak. People raised to fear the wrong book may distrust their own curiosity. It takes more than a law to reverse that. It takes a generation of practice before a culture rediscovers the joy and labor of reading sacred texts with agency.

Why did some leaders defend restrictions in good faith?

Not all gatekeepers were cynics. Some were pastors who had seen what happens when a charismatic reader cherry picks verses to justify cruelty. Some were scholars who worried that a clumsy translation would cause more confusion than clarity. Some thought gradual teaching was kinder than plunging a novice into apocalyptic riddles. Understanding those motives does not excuse excess, but it explains how repression can grow in an institution that also produces charity, art, and law.

The best of those leaders wanted coherence and care. The worst wanted control. The system often could not tell the difference until it was too late.

What changed the balance: technology, markets, and courage

Three forces broke the chokehold.

1. **Technology:** Movable type placed Bibles on tables that once held only bread and salt. Type also standardized spelling and encouraged literacy.

2. **Markets:** Demand for vernacular texts created supply. When families discover that Sunday makes more sense if they can review the passages in their own words, a market appears, and printers follow the silver.

3. **Courage:** Translators and readers accepted risk. Some fled, some hid, some argued in courts until a new equilibrium formed.

None of this was automatic. Gains were uneven and reversible. Yet once a reading public learns to compare texts and challenge footnotes, a different relationship to authority grows. The pulpit remains important. It no longer stands alone.

Returning to the hidden shelf: what the rediscovery of ancient texts teaches now

The twentieth-century discovery of Coptic codices in Egypt did not launch a new church. What it did was puncture the notion that the past was simple. It showed that early Christians argued in rich ways about knowledge, salvation, leadership, and practice. It reminded modern readers that suppression worked, because many of these writings survived only by accident, sealed in jars to escape destruction. The Gospel of Truth reads like a homily on knowledge rather than a chronicle, and that alone complicates tidy textbook outlines about what a gospel must be.

The Gospel of Thomas, terse and provocative, challenges the idea that all formative teaching must arrive in story form. Its sayings invite us to take responsibility for interpretation rather than outsource the task to a chain of authorities. That posture is both exhilarating and risky, which is exactly why later leaders preferred to keep such texts out of reach.

The Gospel of Mary preserves an internal dispute about who may speak, with Mary's wisdom affirmed by some and rejected by others. The scene holds a mirror to any community that claims never to have struggled over a woman's voice. It shows that suppression is not just about ink. It is also about who gets to hold the book while speaking.

The anatomy of a ban: how a single verse can start a fire

To see suppression up close, follow the life of a contested verse in a translation.

A translator chooses a bold but defensible rendering. It circulates in pamphlets before a full Bible edition. Preachers quote it. A bishop hears reports that the new wording undermines a favorite doctrine or punctures a cherished proof text. He convenes a review panel. The panel looks at rival renderings and declares that the new version violates tradition or grammar. The printer is warned to cease distribution. Copies are seized. A public burning takes place to dramatize the decision. The translator is summoned. If he recants, he is assigned to safer tasks. If he refuses, penalties escalate.

Underneath that ritual lies a principle. Control does not require winning every argument about meaning. It requires the power to define which arguments are allowed in public and which must be kept private within licensed channels.

What to look for in official defenses of suppression

Defenses of bans and burnings often rest on three claims, which sound reasonable at first hearing.

1. **Purity:** The faithful need protection from error.

2. **Peace:** The community needs protection from conflict.

3. **Piety:** The holy needs protection from trivialization.

Each claim has a kernel of truth. Yet in practice, they justify the concentration of power. The test is whether leadership can accept robust debate, allow multiple competent translations to coexist, and trust that truth can survive friction. If it cannot, suppression becomes a habit rather than a last resort.

Why this history still matters

Modern readers live after print revolutions and digital abundance. Many can search a verse on a phone in seconds. It is tempting to shrug at old prohibitions as quaint. That would be a mistake.

The deeper lesson is not about a particular language or century. It is about recognizing how institutions manage risk and meaning. Every organization that stewards a sacred text faces the tension between coherence and freedom. The line between teaching and policing is thin. The tools have changed, yet the temptation to control through scarcity, jargon, and credentialing remains.

If you care about ordinary people having a full voice in their own spiritual lives, the antidotes are clear. Teach languages when you can. Share multiple translations without fear. Encourage household readings and neighborhood study circles. Keep official commentaries in their proper place, as companions rather than gatekeepers.

Look back over the terrain we crossed.

First, access was controlled through language, scarcity, and pulpit bottlenecks. Second, disagreement sometimes led to destruction, especially when alternative gospels or bold translations threatened official lines. Third, the arrival of print made control harder, and authorities responded with licensing, seizures, and spectacles of punishment. Fourth, rediscovered texts remind us that early Christian memory was broader than later rules allowed, and that suppression worked precisely because it narrowed the range of what believers knew existed. Finally, the cost of suppression fell not only on books and translators, but on generations of ordinary people who lost habits of agency and the joy of wrestling with the text for themselves.

If you want a single image that captures the whole chapter, picture two scenes. In one, a chained book faces a silent crowd. In the other, a table is covered with open pages, and voices are lively yet charitable. The distance between those scenes is the distance between a faith guarded by fear and a faith confident enough to live with light.

Chapter 10:

Mystical Codes and Hidden Messages – Kabbalah, Bible codes, and esoteric secrets

People do not hide treasures for no reason. They hide them because power pools around what is rare, what is hard to get, and what is easy to misunderstand when stripped of context. The sacred texts of Judaism and early Christianity are not only stories and laws. They are also structured fields of symbolism. Some of those symbols were meant for anyone willing to listen. Other layers were reserved for readers trained to spot the signal inside the noise. This chapter unpacks three streams that often get tangled together in popular talk: the classical Jewish sciences of hidden meaning that grew into Kabbalah, modern claims about Bible codes that scan letters as if they were ciphers, and the esoteric sayings that circulated on the edges of early Christian communities. Along the way, we will keep our eye on the theme of this part of the book: who controls access to meaning, who polices the gates, and how communities decide what counts as truth.

Before we start, a simple agreement between us: nothing here is written to shock. It is written to clarify. If a claim has strong evidence, you will see how it holds. If a claim is alluring yet weak, you will understand why. We will also be clear about what counts as responsible reading versus pattern hunting. That clarity is where serious work begins.

The map under the text: how traditional readers layered meaning

If you open a Torah scroll, you meet consonants written in a hand that has barely changed in more than two thousand years. Classical readers did not treat those lines as a flat surface. They spoke of levels of reading. The well-known acronym PaRDeS summarizes this approach: peshat, the plain sense of the words in context; remez, hints and allusions that link verses together; derash, homiletic expansion that turns verses into teaching for a community; sod, the secret sense that speaks about the structure of reality and the soul. Think of PaRDeS like a staircase. Each step stands on the step below. You do not reach the top by skipping the foundation.

Sod readings moved within a shared grammar. Three devices get mentioned often: gematria, which explores the numeric value of words and the links created by equal sums; notarikon, which treats each letter of a word as the first letter of another word, building compact acronyms into full phrases; and temurah, which permutes or substitutes letters according to fixed schemes. These were not games for their own sake. They offered a way to talk about correspondences between language, number, and creation. When the tradition says that the world is spoken into being, it is natural that letters and numbers become the tools for describing how things cohere.

Kabbalah, the inner architecture of creation and the soul

Kabbalah takes this layered reading and turns it into an ontology. Imagine a map of how divine energy flows from source into the world,

What to remember about PaRDeS

Keep this in mind when people speak of secrets in scripture: sod does not cancel peshat. It builds on it. Secret readings that contradict the plain sense are not deep; they are sloppy. The best hidden readings make the plain meaning feel more solid, not less.

how it condenses, how it fragments, how it returns. The ten sefirot are the best-known elements of that map. They outline qualities through which creation is sustained: crown, wisdom, understanding, lovingkindness, strength, beauty, victory, splendor, foundation, and kingship. Early writers spoke about them with reserve. Later writers drew a tree to visualize their relations, left to right as a play between expansiveness and restraint, top to bottom as stages of manifestation.

Two ideas are central. First, contraction and overflow: to make room for a finite world, infinite presence contracts in a way that allows distinction to appear. That distinction lets mercy and judgment meet without collapse. Second, fracture and repair: vessels that bear the creative light cannot hold all they receive, so they fracture, and sparks of that light scatter into matter. Human action, especially ritual and ethical action, becomes the means by which scattered sparks get lifted and rejoined. This is not a myth to entertain. It is a psychology and an ethics. Where you place your attention, how you use speech, how you take or refuse power, all of that either scatters or gathers.

A reader trained inside this frame engages scripture with an ear for structure. When a number repeats, when a name carries a known value, when parallel stories bend toward one another, the reader listens for resonance. The point is not to force the text to say something new each time. The point is to consent to a discipline where small details are weighted, counted, and woven into a pattern that supports life.

TREE OF LIFE — GEOMETRIC BLUEPRINT

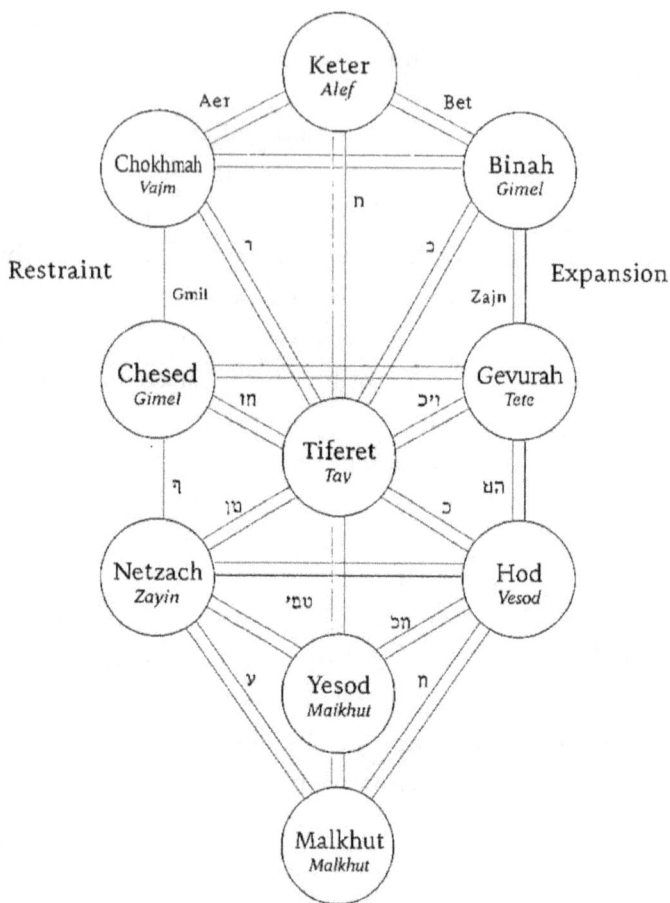

Paths label Alef—Tav, pillars:
Restraint, Balance, Expansion

Working examples that stay inside tradition

1. A word with a value that matches another keyword invites a
   sustained comparison, not a proof of identity. If the value of a
   name equals the value of a phrase that names a divine quality,

the reader explores how that character channels or distorts that quality in the narrative.

2. A numerical pattern that repeats across stories suggests a shared theme. Forty repeats with cycles of trial and transformation: days of flood, years in the wilderness, days on a mountain, days of temptation. This is not a code. It is a way the tradition marks passages from one state to another.

3. A triad of virtues can be traced across legal and narrative material, then aligned with three sefirot, and then turned into practice. For instance, kindness, boundaries, beauty. The last one is not cosmetics; it is the harmony created by the first two in correct proportion.

These are disciplined moves. They are not shortcuts around hard philology, history, and law. They do not ask you to close one eye. They ask you to open both.

Letter grids and statistical secrets, what Bible codes claim and what they do not

The twentieth century saw a different proposal about hidden messages. Instead of reading whole words and sentences, some writers proposed that one could scan scripture as a large letter field, skip letters at fixed intervals, and find names and events hidden in equidistant letter sequences. In theory, any long enough text will yield patterns if you are allowed to search with enough freedom. In practice, the argument for Bible codes rests on two claims: that meaningful clusters appear so often and so tightly that chance is an unlikely explanation, and that these clusters carry advance knowledge of events.

There are simple questions to ask if you want to separate method from myth.

First, how were the rules set before the search began? If you can pick any interval you like, in any direction, across flexible shapes, you will find something that looks impressive. Set the rules in advance, apply them consistently, and the field narrows.

Second, what baseline did you use? If you can find similar clusters in War and Peace or in a newspaper corpus, the claim of uniqueness weakens. If your control texts are not matched in length and letter distribution, your baseline is not serious.

Third, what exactly counts as a hit? If near misses get counted, or if multiple spellings are allowed after the fact, the test is not fair. If you only publish the successful clusters and never report null results, you select the evidence.

Fourth, what you expected before you looked. If you search for terms that everyone talks about, then celebrate when you find them, but you have not tested anything beyond your desire to be amazed.

A more responsible way to think about letter structure is to recall how ancient scribes guarded transmission. They counted letters and words to keep a standard. They trained readers to chant the text with precise vowels and accents recorded in a careful system. That system is a quality control device, not a mystical overlay. It protects the base on which all later interpretation depends. Where modern code hunting treats the text like a cryptogram, the tradition treated it like a living instrument that needs tuning.

What letters can and cannot do

Letters can be counted to preserve a standard text. Letters can be weighed inside a shared symbolic grammar. Letters cannot predict the stock market, give you tomorrow's headlines, or replace the hard work of historical understanding. When claims leap from letters to prophecy without discipline, you are not seeing a secret; you are seeing apophenia, the mind's tendency to find faces in clouds.

Hidden teaching in early Christianity: sayings, disputes, and the politics of memory

Esoteric work did not end at the edge of the Hebrew canon. In the first centuries of the common era, multiple Christian groups collected, repeated, and debated sayings and stories of Jesus. Some circles favored public preaching and clear rules for communal life. Others treasured compact sayings that demanded reflection, and dialogues where a question from a student is followed by an answer that points beyond itself.

One collection, a bare sequence of sayings, cultivates an inner ear. It opens with the promise that the one who grasps the meaning of these sayings will not taste death. This is not a promise of escape from biology. It is a claim that true understanding breaks the cycle of fear and forgetfulness that makes us live as if we were already dead. Many of the sayings work like a mirror. They reflect the reader's present condition. If you bring forth what is within you, what you bring forth will save you. If you do not bring it forth, what you do not bring forth will destroy you. That is a diagnosis, not a riddle.

Another strand presents a female disciple who asks pointed questions, recalls what was taught in private, and encourages the rest when they are shattered by grief or confusion. Her presence is not a novelty stunt. It shows that insight is not a property of a rank or a gender. That insight, however, is not welcomed by everyone. Some resist the idea that she could have received private teaching. Others, more generous, step in to test and then affirm her account. The deeper lesson is simple: communities often measure authority by visibility and office, while wisdom may flow through a different channel. When the two collide, you learn who values truth more than control.

A third work reads like a homily that circles around a single contrast: ignorance versus knowledge of the Father. Ignorance breeds fear, error, and a world shaped by copies of truth rather than by truth itself.

Knowledge is not information you can memorize. It is a transformation that restores you to your source and makes you taste joy. In that account, the life and death of Jesus are not treated as a puzzle to decode. They are presented as an act that attaches a deed of freedom to the cross, a gift that cancels the paperwork of forgetfulness. The conclusion is not coded. It is clear. Those who wake up rediscover themselves and act from that clarity.

Read together, these strands show three pressures working at once. There is pressure to protect the heart of the message from political capture. There is pressure to produce clarity for communities that need rules and leaders. There is pressure to sift testimony, especially testimony that arrives through unexpected voices. The result is a canon for public life and a shadow library for private work. The shadow is not sinister. It is simply the place where intense medicine is stored and handled with care.

Why esoteric traditions guard the gate

Powerful ideas get simplified when they travel. If you open the door wide with no training, you risk melting experience into slogans. Kabbalistic teachers used parables for a reason. They knew that improper use of images, like contraction and broken vessels, could lead to speculation without ethics. Early Christian writers held some conversations inside small circles for a reason. They knew that hints about the divine name and the structure of the inner life could be twisted into magic by hearers who wanted control more than union.

Gatekeeping is not always oppression. Sometimes it is medicine stewardship. That said, gatekeeping can slide into control that protects status rather than souls. The line between care and control is measured by outcomes. Does a teacher's caution produce deeper humility and service in students? Or does it collapse into a monopoly on interpretation that punishes honest questions? Sober traditions tell you to test the fruit. If the fruit is fear and dependency, the tree is sick. If the fruit is greater responsibility, joy, and love for truth, the tree is healthy.

How to read like an insider without joining a clique

You can honor the best of the esoteric tradition without turning it into a club.

Start with grammar and history. Learn how the text says what it says. You cannot read at the secret level if you have not learned the plain sense of the words. Pick one book and know it in its own voice before you stack it with others.

Practice correspondences with restraint. If you find a numeric match, treat it as an invitation to study, not as proof that closes the case. If you find a repeated image across books, ask how it functions in each place before you draw conclusions.

Keep ethics at the center. If a reading makes you clever and leaves you no kinder, it has failed. If a reading makes you more responsible, more patient, and more courageous, it is doing the work that secrets were meant to do.

Refuse the thrill of prediction. Codes that promise to reveal the future will keep you anxious, not awake. The point of hidden teaching is to see the present without illusion, then act.

Hold paradox without panic. Traditions mature by holding truth in tension, for instance, unity and distinction, mercy and judgment, knowledge and humility. Your task is not to flatten these tensions. Your task is to live them without splitting.

The politics of meaning: who decides what counts

No chapter on hidden teaching is complete without facing the social dimension. Meaning is never free of institutions. Scribes copy texts and set standards. Rabbis teach methods and draw lines. Bishops set boundaries for communities. Reformers push back. Mystics go quiet, or they gather in small circles, or they cause waves. Each of these moves is political. Not party politics. The politics of authority, legitimacy, and trust.

Suppression can be frank, as when a text is publicly condemned and destroyed. Suppression can be soft, as when a literary voice is ignored in favor of a more convenient narrative. Sometimes the suppression is even self-inflicted. A community may hide its own hardest teachings because it cannot protect them from misuse. The result is the same. Later readers inherit a landscape where some trails are paved and signposted, while other paths are faint.

The question for us is practical. How do we read across these gaps without romanticizing what was marginalized and without sanctifying what survived? The answer is method. Put patient philology next to contemplative practice. Put historical awareness next to symbolic intelligence. Use both to weigh claims. When a text speaks about an inner light, do not treat it as vapor. Ask how that theme develops across sources. When a text presents a disciple who receives private instruction, do not treat that as a scandal. Ask how communities negotiated teaching that was partly public and partly private. When a text uses the word knowledge, do not reduce it to information. Measure it against the lived transformation that the tradition expects.

A tour of disciplined practice, step by step

Here is a practice path that respects both scholarship and sod.

Step one: choose a passage that matters. A psalm that you pray, an ethical law that you wrestle with, a parable that will not leave you alone. Read it in your primary language, then consult the original words with a lexicon. Note repeated words and echoes.

Step two, anchor the plain sense. Who is speaking? What is the setting? What does the passage ask the hearer to do? Write a short paragraph that anyone could agree with. If you cannot write that paragraph, pause.

Step three, listen for remez. Use cross-references created by the tradition. See where your words appear elsewhere. Watch for images that link chapters across the canon.

Step four, craft a derash. Turn the text into teaching for your present life and community with integrity. Do not bend the verse to your will. Let it cut you first.

Step five, open a door to sod. Here, you may use gematria or a known symbolic mapping. If a number, letter, or image opens into a deeper structure, walk in slowly. Ask what ethical demand this structure makes. If the structure does not shape your life, close the door and return to steps one through four.

Step six, test the fruit. Did this reading increase your love for truth? Did it lessen your fear? Did it widen your patience? If not, return to step two.

A Disciplined Sod Practice

PaRDeS study checklist

1 Choose a passage that matters   *Notes:* _____

2 Anchor the plain sense   *Notes:* _____

3 Listen for remez   *Notes:* _____

4 Craft a derash _____   *Notes:* _____

5 Open a door to sod   *Notes:* _____

6 Test the fruit _____   *Notes:* _____

Peshat, Remez, Derash, Sod

Case studies that respect the text

Case study one: a short phrase that links two worlds. The phrase face to face appears in different zones of scripture. In one, it reports a unique intimacy between a prophet and the divine. In another, it names the dream of a future union. In a symbolic frame, the phrase invites a meditation on the sefirot as divine face presented to human face, then asks for an ethical imitation where people meet face to face with truth and kindness. Nothing occult is required. The symbol simply connects vision and practice.

Case study two, a saying about light. A saying tells you that there is light within a person of light, and if that person does not give the light, it is dark. The plain sense is clear. Your task is to become what you already are in potential. The symbolic sense ties that inner light to scattered sparks that call for gathering. The ethical sense ties the same line to speech and action that either spreads darkness or increases light. The political sense observes how communities respond to people who become light sources without permission. Some welcome the light. Others try to shade it.

Case study three, a grief-filled scene that turns into courage. A small circle is thrown into confusion. One voice recalls what was taught, turns grief into purpose, faces down scorn, and strengthens the group. The plain sense is pastoral. The symbolic sense reads the scene as a repair where harmonious balance rises between mercy and truth. The political sense notes resistance to a voice that does not fit a preferred profile. The ethical sense challenges you to step forward when your memory and insight are needed.

What to do with modern claims of hidden prophecies

You will meet people who say they have found events coded in the text. Meet them with respect and firmness. Ask for preregistered methods, fair baselines, and clear definitions of success. Ask whether the discovery helps anyone live with more courage and love. If a code gains followers because it flatters the in-group as seers, it does not serve the purposes of scripture. If a code turns minds toward fear and speculation, it is not a healing secret. Let those tests guide your response.

How suppression works in practice, and how truth survives

Suppression is rarely a cartoon of villains burning books. It happens in small choices. A teacher refuses to endorse a commentary, so students stop copying it. A community that values external order more than interior work marginalizes those who practice intense prayer and symbolic reading. A political leader joins a theological camp, so texts that support rivals get less oxygen. Over time, entire streams become hard to find.

Yet the truth has a habit of leaking. Manuscripts are buried and later found. A saying survives in a rival collection. A story whispered in one century becomes a printed page in another. When the material resurfaces, you face two temptations. You can romanticize the hidden as purer than the public. You can demonize the public as mere control. Both moves are lazy. The more courageous move is to weigh each text by the same scales, its coherence with the core, the fruit it yields, its capacity to hold paradox without violence.

The lived point of hidden work

A simple rule will keep you oriented. If an interpretation increases love of God and neighbor and deepens your sense of responsibility, it belongs. If it increases contempt, pride, or a taste for power over others, it does not. Secrets exist to create solid people, not insiders who collect hints like trophies. The inner path is not rare because it hides in code. It is rare because it asks for patience, truthfulness, and joy under pressure.

The most subversive thing a hidden teaching can do is to make you unbribable, hard to flatter, governed by conscience, and free of the need to control other people's consciences. That kind of person is hard to manage. Institutions that prefer compliance will feel threatened. Communities that love truth will feel relieved. This is where power, control, and suppression meet the most practical outcome of mystical work. The secrets are not toys, and they are not riddles to crack. They are tools for building people who cannot be bought.

Closing counsel

Study the grammar, honor the story, practice the ethics, and let the symbols do their quiet work. Avoid shortcuts. Avoid thrills. Refuse the trap of control. Choose the patient's joy of learning to read across levels. If you do that, you will be able to engage Kabbalah without superstition, assess Bible code claims without cynicism, and recognize genuine esoteric secrets without being captured by secrecy.

Part IV — Echoes of Forbidden Truth

Chapter 11: The Books That Are Still Missing – Clues to scriptures yet to be found

Let us begin with a simple, unsettling fact: the ancient world copied scriptures by hand, page by page, on materials that tear, rot, and vanish. When history depends on fibers and ink, gaps are guaranteed. Our task in this chapter is to treat those gaps like archaeological sites, to read the negative space, and to map the patterns that hint at writings still missing. We will listen carefully to the clues left by recovered works, by titles preserved in lists, by quotations in rival writings, and by the physical scars inside codices. We will not romanticize the unknown; we will interrogate it.

This chapter moves in three beats. First, we will learn how known discoveries point toward what has not yet surfaced. Second, we will trace concrete case studies, including the tantalizing losses inside specific codices. Third, we will turn method into strategy, showing how to recognize the fingerprints of a missing source when all you have is a residue of quotations, a sudden shift of voice, or a title that survived without its text.

Evidence of worm damage

Nag Hammadi: Jar and Coptic Codices (Upper Egypt, 1945)

How recovered books teach us to look for the missing

Every recovered manuscript carries a double message. On the one hand, it gives us a new text. On the other hand, it tells us how and where texts were stored, titled, recopied, bundled, and lost. The story of a codex dug from a jar in Upper Egypt teaches more than its pages say in words. In the mid twentieth century, peasants near Nag Hammadi reportedly unearthed a jar that spilled out a small library of Coptic manuscripts. One volume, later nicknamed the Jung Codex, contained, among other works, a text modern editors call the Gospel of Truth. Even that codex bears a visible absence. Several folios are missing, and the edition that first made the work widely available notes the gap openly. From folio 8 verso to 22 recto, we have a continuous run, then we hit the break. The precise folios that vanished are numbered in the description, and the hole sits right where one would expect conceptual development, a place where lost lines matter. Such lacunae are not an embarrassment. They are evidence, telling us how fragile the chain of custody was, and how to search for corroborating copies elsewhere.

The same discovery cycle shows that a cluster of codices can preserve different genres, from homilies and revelatory dialogues to sayings collections. A sayings gospel attributed to Thomas, preserved in Codex II, contains 114 sayings rather than a narrative, and its discovery context is described with care, including the findspot near Khenoboskion and the language, Sahidic Coptic. When one manuscript preserves sayings without a story, that very absence suggests older sources behind our canonical narratives. The cluster of texts also reveals an editorial habit: communities gathered diverse writings that made sense to them together. Once you grasp how an ancient library was curated, you can infer what other titles might have once sat beside the ones we have.

Missing within the found: when a book announces its own losses

Sometimes the best guide to missing books is the hole sitting inside a book we can hold. A clear example is the Gospel of Mary. Three incomplete manuscripts survive. The largest, a Coptic translation often called the Berlin Codex, was recovered from a Christian burial context near Panopolis. The codex itself gathered several works, and the Gospel of Mary portion is damaged. Nineteen pages once existed. Only nine pages remain, and the opening and a section in the middle are lost. The missing pages matter because they likely contained both framing dialogue and parts of Mary's revelation. Two earlier Greek fragments, copied in the third century and found at Oxyrhynchus, overlap and confirm that we are dealing with a Greek original that circulated beyond Egypt. The point is simple: the Gospel of Mary teaches us how to think about the missing by showing where its own flesh was torn away.

Why does this matter for the broader hunt? Because the title of this work is not neutral. A gospel bearing a woman's name is an outlier in early Christian titling practices, which overwhelmingly preferred male names or groups. The very fact that a gospel bore Mary's name signals a community that accepted a woman's teaching authority, a stance that other groups resisted. When you see the politics encoded in a title, you can predict that parallel books existed, were contested, and could have been suppressed or simply left unrecopied. This is a behavioral clue, not a conspiracy theory. It tells you which shelves to search and which networks to study.

When a polemical opponent preserves a ghost

Another clue comes from cross-references. The Gospel of Truth is a telling example. A second-century writer reported that a group cherished a work by that title. Centuries later, a Coptic codex turns up with a text that fits the name and theology. That match between an outsider's report and an insider's book is not just satisfying, it is methodological gold. It validates the habit of taking titles mentioned in external sources seriously, then checking libraries and fragment collections for a match. It also proves that some books that sound hypothetical are very real. If one hostile witness preserves a title that later reappears in a codex, then other hostile witnesses likely hide similar clues.

Where to look for the next finds

The pattern of discovery itself becomes a guide. Small caches, desert dryness, and monastic libraries have been unusually kind to fragile papyrus and parchment. The Nag Hammadi find, described as a jar burial in a zone of ancient monastic activity, shows the value of liminal spaces: burial grounds, hermit cells, outbuildings near monasteries, and cliff face niches. The Berlin Codex came from a Christian burial place near Panopolis, again pointing to funerary contexts as protective environments for books. The Oxyrhynchus fragments teach the value of ancient dumping grounds that preserve papyri from every walk of life, including religious texts. When you put these patterns together, you get a practical search map.

Case study: The Gospel of Mary, what the gaps reveal

The preserved sections of the Gospel of Mary lay out a post-resurrection dialogue in which Mary addresses and encourages the disciples, and they preserve a dispute about whether the Savior would have revealed privately to a woman what he did not tell male disciples. The surviving text shows Mary as a teacher and interpreter, then shows some male disciples resisting her role. The scene ends with one of the men defending Mary's authority and urging the group to preach. The missing pages at the front likely carried framing material and possibly a scene that anchored Mary's authority in an encounter with the risen Jesus. This is not speculation for its own sake. The title confirms the preserved narrative of Mary's leadership. A missing beginning that introduced her would fit the book's overall design.

The same work also makes a broader historical point. It is the only known early gospel named after a woman, which tells us that certain Christian groups did not merely tolerate women as patrons or witnesses. They treated a woman's teaching as gospel grade material. That decision was controversial in other settings. The title itself was a boundary marker. Wherever you see a line that stark, you can expect writings on both sides of that line, some of which will be missing. The Gospel of Mary, incomplete as it is, signals a whole shelf of texts that centered women's teaching that either did not survive or have not yet come to light.

Mary Teaching in a First-Century House Gathering

Case study, the Gospel of Truth, a title that returned from rumor

When the Coptic Gospel of Truth surfaced, scholars immediately recognized the title from an early catalogue of heresies. The codex itself is fourth century, but the work it transmits is older. The editor who described it in the mid twentieth century could already note concrete features like the manuscript page range, the dialect, and the missing folios. These are not trivial bibliographic notes. Together, they tell us that titles can survive centuries as accusations and then reappear as manuscripts. They also show that partial survival is normal. A missing pair of folios can interrupt an argument in mid-flight. When that happens, cross reading is mandatory. You read parallel passages elsewhere in the work for terminology and metaphors that might have spanned the gap. You also search other codices for duplicate copies.

The lesson for missing scriptures is straightforward. You respect titles preserved by opponents, then you scour codices for a match, knowing that lacunae are likely.

Case study, the Gospel of Thomas, how a sayings book implies a source

A narrative gospel tells a story, a sayings gospel strings logia like beads. The Gospel of Thomas is the purest surviving example of the sayings genre from early Christianity, preserving 114 sayings attributed to Jesus and framed as the work of Judas Didymus Thomas. The discovery report emphasizes its place in the Nag Hammadi cache, the language, and the striking choice to skip narrative. That choice is itself a clue. If one community circulated a sayings collection in Coptic in the fourth century, the traditions behind it could be older, and other sayings collections may have existed in Greek or Aramaic that perished. The presence of an aphoristic tradition in one book is a fingerprint for absent cousins. Where a sayings book survived, look for quotation seams in narrative gospels that hint at a shared source. Where aphorisms come in clusters in other texts, consider that they may all reach back to a now-lost collection. This is how a found text becomes a guide to a missing one.

Six practical ways scholars reconstruct the unseen

1. **Title tracking across hostile sources:** If an early critic mentions a title, note it, then hunt for it in codices and fragment catalogues. The Gospel of Truth is the model of this method working.

2. **Lacuna mapping inside codices:** Note where leaves are missing, then analyze whether narrative logic requires content of a certain kind in that gap. The Gospel of Mary's opening and mid-book losses are a textbook case.

3. **Genre inference:** When a sayings collection survives, infer that other sayings collections once existed. When a revelation dialogue survives, assume sister dialogues once circulated, possibly with different leading voices.

4. **Title politics:** Treat striking titles as programmatic. A gospel centered on a woman's teaching is a signal, not an accident. Expect parallel works from the same circle and counter works from critics.

5. **Manuscript sociology:** Follow the communities that stored and copied texts. Monastic peripheries, burial contexts, and provincial towns were not marginal for preservation; they were decisive.

6. **Overlap reading:** When two fragments overlap a stretch of text, collate them to triangulate what an earlier exemplar may have contained, then note where neither preserves the opening. That gap is not empty. It identifies a likely place to find authorial ascription and narrative setup.

What early clusters tell us about missing clusters

Take the library contexts we have. The Berlin Codex joins the Gospel of Mary with three other writings. The Nag Hammadi cache clusters revelatory dialogues and meditative works in codices that feel curated rather than random. These clusters show intellectual families. They imply that when one work survived, its siblings once traveled with it. If two siblings are present and one is gone, do not assume it never existed. Assume it was not recopied, or that its last copy was too damaged to survive. Then you search for its echo in quotations, summaries, and reworkings inside other texts from the same cluster.

Predictable missing books that still make sense to seek

Given the patterns above, what missing writings remain logically plausible targets for future discovery or reconstruction?

a) A fuller Mary corpus.

The Gospel of Mary demonstrates a community ready to center a woman teacher. The surviving narrative shows Mary interpreting, encouraging, and defending her authority against skeptical male colleagues. That combination makes it reasonable to expect sister works in the same orbit, perhaps shorter dialogues or collections of sayings credited to Mary. The missing front leaves of the Gospel of Mary may even have named a companion text. Whether such works survive is unknown. The logic of the title and the role of Mary suggest they once existed.

b) Parallel titles hinted by polemic.

A title like the Gospel of Truth, known first from an opponent's catalogue, proves that hostile lists can hide real book names. Other titles that show up in such lists should be treated as live possibilities, not fictions, and should be matched against codex inventories and fragment registries. The principle is solid. The case study already worked.

c) More sayings collections.

Once a sayings gospel such as Thomas exists, other communities could have compiled different selections, either earlier or later, some more ascetic, some more mystical, some more congregational. Short aphoristic sequences inside narrative gospels could be the tip of an iceberg. The survival of 114 sayings in one book, without a story, tells us a mode of preservation that invites additional examples.

How disputes on the page expose lost backstories

The Gospel of Mary preserves a scene of conflict over authority. A man voices the suspicion that the Savior would not reveal privately to a woman what he did not disclose to men, and another man rebukes him and affirms Mary's worth. That exchange did not appear out of nowhere. It implies that some communities already valued Mary's teaching, others did not, and texts moved in and out of favor along this fault line. If you are hunting for missing writings, follow the fault. Works that defend one side of an argument presuppose that the other side has its own literature. Even if that literature is now gone, you can reconstruct its stance by how it is answered.

Reading the negative space inside a damaged page

Missing front leaves often carry prologues, reasons for writing, and attributions. When those leaves are gone, you focus on what remains. In the Gospel of Mary, the narrator's sympathy is obvious. The narrator knows more than an objective recorder and favors Mary's interpretation. When a narrator shows a preference, that preference is itself a relic of a broader program. It suggests the missing opening likely framed Mary as a bearer of true teaching, not a novelty. A missing prologue is not a dead end. It is a cue to read every surviving thread for how it assumes Mary's status. That is how you let the text itself help you fill the gap without inventing content.

Material culture clues that narrow the hunt

The Nag Hammadi codices are in a particular Coptic dialect, which points to the copying environment. The Gospel of Truth copy is dated paleographically to the fourth century, with careful caveats about the window of time. The Gospel of Thomas translation emphasizes the amphoras and the sands, the monastic presence nearby, and the language used. The Gospel of Mary's Coptic copy was found in a niche in a wall in a Christian burial context, wrapped in feathers, a detail that tells you about ritual care and environmental protection. These concrete facts turn into search heuristics. If a region yields Sahidic codices from a monastic zone, you weigh that zone heavily for further survey. If a volume traveled far from its point of composition, you trace the routes.

How to use overlaps and cross copies to revive the missing

The Gospel of Mary survives in one longer Coptic copy and two short Greek fragments. The overlap lets us test translations, confirms the Greek original, and shows scribal variation. It also creates a triangulation effect. If the Greek fragments preserve a middle section and an ending, and the Coptic preserves a middle and an end with different gaps, then the absence is narrowed. You can usually say which pages are missing, not just that something is gone. That precision matters when new fragments surface. You know where they would fit. You can also recognize a misattributed scrap by its vocabulary and expected sequence.

What would missing scriptures look like if we found them?

If another gospel centered on a woman teacher surfaced, we would expect several markers already visible in the Gospel of Mary. A sympathetic narrator, a revelatory dialogue format, a scene of opposition and vindication, and a title that names the woman. We would also expect the work to share thematic vocabulary with sibling texts from the same intellectual family, not because one copied the other, but because they breathed the same air.

If a second work titled like the Gospel of Truth appeared, we would expect it to fit an existing theological stream and to echo metaphors, especially knowledge and joy language, with a strong emphasis on revelation as the cure for ignorance. We would also expect gaps. The missing is part of the package.

If another sayings collection surfaced, we would expect aphorisms without narrative glue, possibly with a short incipit naming a collector.

The number of sayings might differ, and the theology might be less or more ascetic. What would unite the genre is the confidence that short sayings carry, transforming power.

The discipline that keeps us honest

Working with missing scriptures is not a license to invent. It is a discipline. You proceed by chains of inference that are public, repeatable, and anchored in manuscripts we actually possess. You watch how titles behave. You catalog where codices were found. You note who is allowed to teach inside a text and who objects. You align fragments. You resist the urge to fill the silence with wishful thinking. The thrill of discovery is real, but so is the craft of restraint.

What the missing can already teach us

The missing is not empty. The Gospel of Mary has already shown us that a woman in the earliest generations is presented as a teacher and interpreter. That message does not depend on the lost pages. It is visible in what remains. The Gospel of Truth has already shown that works mentioned by opponents can and do reappear in codices centuries later. That vindication does not need the missing folios to make its point. The Gospel of Thomas has already shown that a sayings tradition stood on its own, which makes room for more such collections, whether or not we ever find them. These three facts, drawn from three different works, already revise the story of early Christian literature.

Building a practical checklist for future work

Here is a tight, field-ready set of actions for anyone engaged in the hunt.

- **Follow the titles.** Cross-index titles that hostile writers list with actual codex tables of contents. The Gospel of Truth is the proven case.

- **Map the codex.** Photograph and diagram which leaves are missing, then infer what content would likely fall there, given the work's logic.
- **Profile the narrator.** Decide whose side the narrator is on. In the Gospel of Mary, the narrator's stance is part of the evidence.
- **Use overlaps ruthlessly.** Collate fragment overlaps, even when they seem small. Over time, they become anchors.
- **Search the margins.** Survey monastic outskirts, burial niches, and ancient refuse sites where the climate is kind to papyrus.
- **Expect a family, not a singleton.** Where one revelatory dialogue survives, expect sisters. Where one saying book survives, expect others.

Closing the gap between imagination and evidence

Forbidden history is not a license to fantasize. It is a promise that careful readers can recover more than they expect from what is already in hand. The missing will always be larger than the found. Yet the findings already speak with surprising volume about the books we still lack. One gospel with a woman's name points to an entire horizon of women's voices that were not copied endlessly, yet were strong enough to survive in one codex. One title revived from a heresiologist's list proves that rumor can become manuscript. One saying book assures us that the earliest tradition could circulate without narrative, which multiplies the places we can expect older sayings to surface.

We are not done. The desert keeps its secrets well, but it does not keep them forever. A jar waits under a collapsed wall. A niche is still hidden behind plaster. A few fibers lie in a box, misfiled, with the line we need. The way to honor the missing is to read the found with enough care that, when the next fragment appears, we will recognize it for what it is.

Chapter 12:

Why These Texts Matter Today – Faith, freedom, and the power of hidden words

Y ou pick up a fragment, you read a few lines, and suddenly the room feels larger than its walls. That is what hidden words do. They give the present a bigger horizon, they reopen questions a culture had quietly closed, and they hand ordinary people a language for courage. This chapter is about that power. It is about why long-buried writings like the Gospel of Mary, the Gospel of Truth, and the Gospel of Thomas matter now, not as museum pieces, but as living tools for faith and freedom.

These texts do not demand that you become someone else to approach God. They invite you to become fully human, awake, responsible, and free. They push back on spiritual fear with understanding, on gatekeeping with conscience, on cynicism with a stubborn joy. In them, ignorance is the real prison, knowledge is medicine, and love is a practiced skill, not a sentiment. In a time hungry for trustworthy authority yet suspicious of control, their voice is surprisingly contemporary.

The case for hidden words in a loud age

Modern life is noisy. It offers instant opinions, swift judgments, and a strange fatigue that comes from being over-informed and under-formed. The hidden words argue for the opposite rhythm. One text, known since antiquity as the Gospel of Truth, frames the whole spiritual problem as ignorance of the Source, which breeds anxiety and terror. The remedy is not louder rules; it is knowledge of the Father that brings relief like daylight to a nightmare, and it yields joy, not dread. In that telling, Jesus is the teacher who turns even his crucifixion into a teaching, a fruit offered for people to taste, so that their fear might be changed into understanding and life.

That is not a soft message. It is a direct challenge to any religious style that keeps people dependent, frightened, or small. If the root problem is ignorance, then the task of faith is education in the richest sense: awakening, formation, and practice. The Gospel of Truth sketches this as a healing of forgetfulness, a sobering from drunkenness, and a gradual return to unity that replaces confusion.

Faith without fear, conscience without chains

The Gospel of Thomas is blunt about the culture of gatekeepers. One of its sayings remembers religious experts who held the keys of knowledge, did not go in themselves, and hindered others who wanted to go in. That is not anti-faith; that is a physician's diagnosis of a real disease: spiritual control that blocks spiritual growth. The remedy is not to burn down the house; it is to give the keys back to the people, to teach seekers how to walk in.

Thomas also refuses the temptation to postpone the divine into a later, safer place. Asked when the kingdom will come, the answer is startling: it will not arrive by watching for it, no one will be able to point and say "here" or "there," since it is spread out over the whole earth, and people do not see it. That line, if you let it sit with you during a commute, in a clinic waiting room, at a workbench, or on a hard wooden pew, will slowly recalibrate your day. It shifts the focus from hunting for holy places to training for holy perception.

A woman who stands up, and why that still matters

One of the fiercest scenes in early Christian literature is not a miracle story; it is a conversation after the trauma of crucifixion. The disciples are wrecked, frightened, and grieving. Mary stands up, steadies them, and reminds them of what they have been prepared to do. She repeats the teaching she received: do not add new burdens, do not multiply laws, announce the good news, and trust the presence that dwells within. She reframes sorrow as a mission. That is leadership.

The pushback is immediate. Andrew doubts the content. Peter doubts the legitimacy. He questions whether the Teacher would ever have spoken privately with a woman, whether men should sit and listen to her, and whether she was chosen above them. The argument is not over a footnote; it is over who is allowed to speak. The text knows that power often hides behind piety. It gives that behavior a name. Then it does something bolder: it has Levi step in to defend Mary, to shame Peter's hot temper, and to insist that if the Savior has made her worthy, no one else gets to undo that call.

This is not abstract theory. The Gospel of Mary portrays a community wrestling with grief, authority, and gender. It shows how quickly fear can become policing, and how necessary it is to have allies who refuse that turn. It also shows Mary's teaching content, not just her courage. She passes on a vision about the soul's ascent past four Powers and seven faces of Wrath, naming Darkness, Desire, and Ignorance as the inner adversaries that confuse and enslave. The soul answers each one with the intelligence of experience, and moves toward Rest and Silence. That is the kind of spirituality people can use in a hard week, and it comes from the mouth of a woman the text honors as a teacher.

Freedom is not lawlessness; it is maturity.

Mary's scene would be dramatic enough as a protest, but it is more than that. It is constructive. Her teaching lays out a spiritual psychology that sounds like the best contemporary wisdom: know how Desire manipulates your attention, learn how Ignorance dresses up as certainty, recognize Wrath when it steals your judgment and calls itself "principle." The aim is not to become an angel; it is to become truly human, to clothe yourself with the complete person, and to live from that center. The text has Levi use that exact phrase, urging the disciples to put on the perfect Human Being and preach the gospel with no extra laws attached. That is an ancient language for adult religion.

The same chapter shows why communities that fear women's leadership fear maturity itself. Treating Mary as a permanent exception keeps everyone else a permanent child. Treating Mary as a prototype presses every disciple, male and female, to grow up. The Gospel of Mary closes on a simple sign that they understood: they began to announce the message. The title, preserved in both Coptic and Greek, leaves no doubt about the authorial intent: a Gospel named after a woman, which is exceptional for the period. That closing detail is not a footnote; it is an instruction.

Vesting the Whole Person

The message of joy, even when life is hard

The Gospel of Truth returns here with a tone many people do not expect from early Christian controversy. It speaks in the register of joy. Knowledge makes people sober and free, yes, but it also makes them glad. These writings do not cultivate grim perfectionism. They cultivate an active, resilient delight in learning how things actually are, and in living accordingly. They compare the change to a drunk person who becomes sober, to someone waking from a bad dream, to a flock learning they are cared for by a real shepherd who notices the one who is missing.

That matters in a period like ours, saturated with outrage. Anger can be useful when it protects the vulnerable, yet it cannot sustain a life. Joy can. Joy is not an anesthetic; it is a competence. In these texts, the competence comes from a steady vision of reality: God is knowable as Source, the Word takes on a body and therefore human experience can be trusted, and the whole aim is union that does not erase difference, it fulfills it. This is why people today who are burnt out on arguments keep finding a home in these materials.

The scandal of equality, then and now

You do not need a long history lesson to see how disruptive the Gospel of Mary's scene is. The text itself tells you. Peter's protest assumes rules about who may teach, how men should behave around women, and how revelation should be controlled. Levi's defense punctures those assumptions by appealing to the same authority Peter claims to honor. It is not that Mary is a token exception; it is that the premise itself is wrong. Men and women share the same Spirit, and both may be called to instruct others. That claim is not only embedded in the dynamics of the conversation, but it is also echoed in other early materials that remember women as bearers of insight.

For modern communities, this is not simply about ordination or titles, important as those are. It is about the deeper habit of deferring to dominance. The hidden words are not content with symbolic wins. They push the whole community toward shared responsibility, toward listening before lecturing, and toward letting reality instruct us even when it insults our customs.

Inner work, outer life

People often worry that attention to inner "knowledge" will produce self-absorption. The best of these texts prevents that error. The Gospel of Thomas keeps the spiritual path grounded in the ordinary through brief, piercing sayings. It urges you to be as alert as serpents and as simple as doves, to pass through the world like travelers, and to recognize that a life rooted in the Source will generate action. The slogans cut cleanly through excuses. They keep you from mistaking complexity for wisdom or busyness for devotion.

The Gospel of Truth ties the inner and outer by insisting that the Word took on a body. That line carries weight. If God's self-expression meets us in flesh, then work in the world matters. Justice work, teaching, caregiving, and neighborliness are not distractions; they are classrooms. The correction of errors is not a war against people; it is patient help for those who are still trapped in forgetting.

Reading Mary's vision as a map for real days

Mary's account of the soul meeting Powers is not a fantasy tale; it is a manual. Darkness is the confusion of value, Desire is the hijacking of attention, Ignorance is the refusal to learn, and Wrath is the heat that makes us feel right while we harm. The soul in Mary's vision answers each with clarity and moves on. This is exactly the work of adult spirituality. You learn to notice when your inner weather is foggy, when an appetite is steering, when pride is pretending to be confidence, and when anger is masquerading as righteousness. You respond, you move, you rest.

Scholars sometimes debate whether Mary describes an ascent after death or an experience now. The text itself points to immediacy. The Powers are encountered in the present, and Rest can be tasted now as grace. The aim is a stable mind, a life that can act from poise rather than react from panic. That is an antidote to our era's cycle of outrage and exhaustion.

No extra chains

A detail in the Gospel of Mary is easy to miss and essential to remember. The instruction to the disciples is simple: announce the good news, impose no law other than what the Teacher witnessed, and do not pile more rules on top of the Torah. Communities often drift in the opposite direction, adding policies to manage every edge case. The hidden words advise restraint. Let the living core do its work, then add only what protects life, not what stifles it.

That conserves spiritual energy. People who spend most of their time enforcing rules have little attention left for teaching, healing, or delight. People who spend their time learning how to see will need fewer rules, because attention itself disciplines the will.

Why these texts matter today

First, they return the initiative to the seeker. You are not a passive recipient of distant authority; you are a participant in a living tradition that expects you to become capable, clear, and compassionate. That is healthy for faith communities and civic life alike.

Second, they expose the mechanisms of control with grace rather than scorn. By showing you exactly how fear, ignorance, and anger operate inside a community and within a person, they train your judgment without making you cynical.

Third, they rehabilitate joy as a serious spiritual practice. Joy is not a mood; it is the fruit of seeing clearly and acting openly. It is both motive and measure.

Fourth, they honor the voices of women not as adornments but as authorities. A Gospel titled after a woman, preserved in multiple languages, is not an accident. It is a statement that is still doing its work.

Fifth, they align with the best of contemporary psychological insight while keeping a theocentric horizon. Desire, Ignorance, and Wrath are named and engaged, not denied. Rest and Silence are named and pursued, not postponed.

A brief field guide for communities

If you are a pastor, teacher, or organizer, you can put these texts to work without changing your logo or your liturgy.

- Teach the difference between fear-based compliance and conscience-based obedience. The Gospel of Truth is your ally here, with its movement from ignorance to knowledge to joy.

- Normalize women teaching men and men learning from women. Use the scene with Mary, Peter, Andrew, and Levi as a case study, then ask what structural habits in your community still echo Peter's anxiety.

- Replace one policy with one practice. Swap a seldom-used rule for a shared exercise, such as a weekly examen that watches for Darkness, Desire, Ignorance, and Wrath, ending with a minute of Silence.

- Preach the already-present kingdom by training attention to the ordinary. Fold Thomas's counsel into pastoral care, reminding the anxious that they do not need to wait for a perfect moment to meet God.

A word about discovery

Part of the modern fascination with these writings is their story of recovery from the sands of Egypt in the twentieth century. That history matters because it mirrors the content: what was hidden is revealed, what was forgotten is remembered, what was feared can be faced. The codices that yielded the Gospel of Truth came to light near Nag Hammadi, and scholars recognized in one of those treatises the very writing earlier polemicists had mocked as "the Gospel of Truth." However, we evaluate dates and dialects; the important thing here is the renewed access to voices that had been sidelined by controversy and time.

What about that hard saying in Thomas

Readers often stumble on Thomas's closing exchange where Peter says Mary should leave the group since women are not worthy of life, and Jesus answers by speaking of making the woman "a man" so that she, too, will enter the kingdom. Do not flatten that line into misogyny or an easy modern answer. Read it against the Gospel of Mary's insistence on the full, shared stature of women and men as complete persons. In early Christian idiom, "becoming a man" can function as a metaphor for maturity, for the integration of qualities that were socially coded as masculine or feminine, into a whole self. The point is not erasure of women, it is the transfiguration of everyone into the complete Human Being that the tradition aims for. The tensions around that language are real, and the Gospel of Mary preserves the argument so that communities can learn to resolve it well.

Putting it all together

The hidden words matter because they make the inner life practical, the outer life humane, and the common life honest. They call out control that wears a holy face. They train discernment without training contempt. They honor women as authors and authorities. They insist that the kingdom is already here, that the task is learning to see and learning to love. They define salvation as the healing of ignorance by knowledge, fear by joy, and isolation by fellowship. In them, Jesus is not a mascot for a team; he is a teacher who hands the tools to anyone who will use them.

The best way to honor these texts is to let them change how we live. Start with Mary's steadiness in the face of grief and suspicion. Continue with Thomas's insistence that the holy is already in the room. Keep the Gospel of Truth's joyful seriousness as your tone. Then go and do the ordinary things with extraordinary attention. That is how hidden words become public blessings.

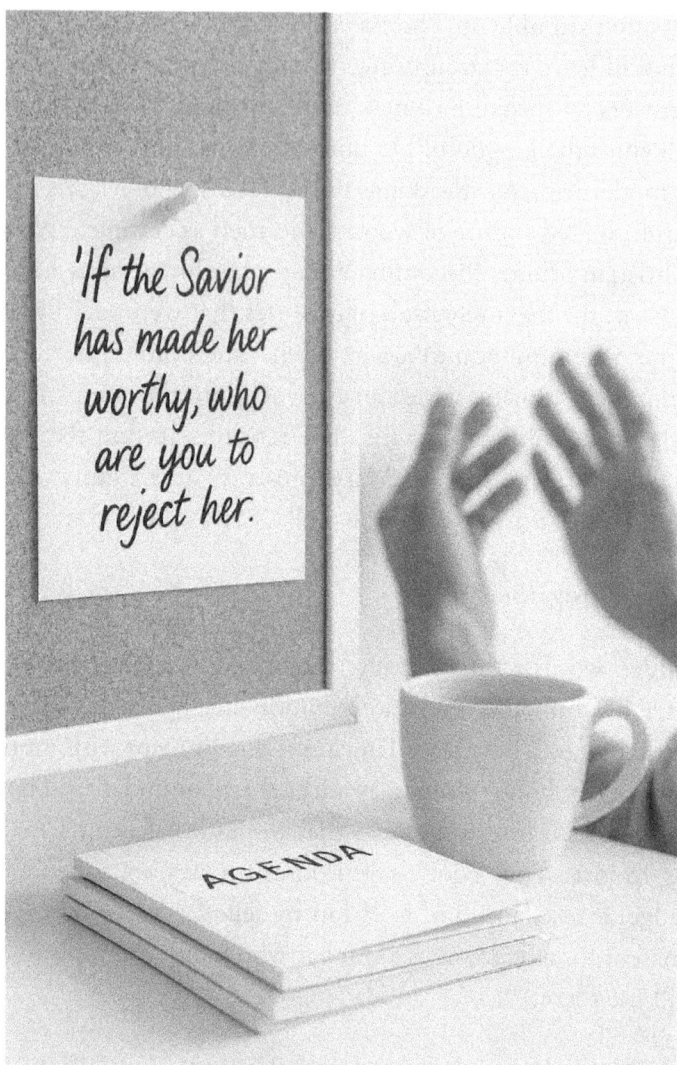

'If the Savior has made her worthy, who are you to reject her.

AGENDA

Conclusion:

The Voice of the Suppressed Scriptures

Close the covers for a moment and listen to what is now in your hands: not a gallery of curiosities, but a recovered conversation about God, conscience, and power. Across these pages, you met knowledge that almost entered public worship, facts that were copied with care, then hidden or ignored, and books that returned from the sand to expose how memory is managed. You met fierce arguments about who may teach, how to test visions, and what counts as knowledge that heals. All of it adds up to a single, stubborn truth: the Bible's world was broader than the playlist that survived, and ordinary people are meant to read widely, weigh wisely, and live bravely.

What began with a scribe choosing which leaf to copy became a tour through rival gospels, visionary tours, and the slow tightening of public reading lists. Your journey showed why some texts thrived near the altar while others learned to survive by going quiet. The mechanics were rarely theatrical. Scarcity, translation costs, pastoral caution, and the need for unity did most of the work, while bonfires and bans supplied the headlines. The result was a center that held, and margins that fell out of view. This is not an invitation to cynicism; it is a call to competence: know how canons form, know how suppression actually works, and then test every claim, whether it comes from a pulpit, a monastery shelf, or a clay jar split open by a farmer's hands.

You now know what the desert gave back. At Nag Hammadi, fourth-century codices preserved second-century thought, including a sayings gospel that trains perception, a homily that treats ignorance as a human disease, and dialogues that put contested authority onstage. The jar was not a conspiracy trophy; it was a time capsule that proved how many early Christians copied and kept writings that did not fit later rules, then hid them when possession became risky. The recovery does not overthrow the center; it widens the room and corrects our habits of hearing.

One voice in particular will not go quiet. In the Gospel of Mary, you watched a woman steadily frighten disciples, teach the discipline of a mind that refuses Darkness, Desire, Ignorance, and Wrath, and face Peter's suspicion with clarity that another disciple finally defends. The issue was not gossip; it was governance: can understanding speak with authority, and can a woman be believed when she carries that understanding? That scene has a long afterlife because it names the real battlefield, not over footnotes, but over who holds the book while speaking.

Another voice worked like a physician. The Gospel of Truth pictured salvation as the cure of fear by knowledge, the waking from a nightmare into joy. It is as if someone told a weary congregation that the cross is not a riddle to admire, it is a fruit to taste, so that terror loosens and courage returns. Read alongside Thomas, which drills attention through brief sayings, the point sharpens: faith without interior formation can be managed from the outside, faith with interior formation grows adults who do not need to be ruled by panic or fashion.

Then there were the visions. Set side by side, the Apocalypse of Peter and the Shepherd of Hermas show how early Christians argued their way to hope. Peter's tour speaks in images that force you to take justice seriously, with a whispered hint that mercy may reach farther than many assume. Hermas turns apocalypse into a building site, a tower rising as people repent, share, and endure, with the deadline near enough to matter, yet delayed for mercy. Both nearly entered the fixed list, both were used for instruction for generations, and both still teach communities how to end well, not by guessing dates, but by telling the truth and doing the work that remains.

If suppression had a face in these pages, it was less a tyrant with a torch and more a system that narrows access by habits: who gets trained to read, which translations are licensed, how archivists label their shelves, which disputes are allowed in public, and when a single eccentric verse becomes a pretext for seizures and burnings. Control is real, yet the book taught you a more useful lesson: truth leaks. A saying migrates into a rival codex. A letter survives as a quotation in a critique. A chest is buried in dry soil and waits. When the pages rise again, the only mature response is the one you practiced here: weigh the text by its coherence with the deep rule, by the fruit it yields, and by its power to make whole people rather than anxious insiders.

This is where the journey lands. The story you inherited was strong, and it will remain strong, precisely because you now know how to read it with the lights on. The recovered writings do not ask you to trade one set of gatekeepers for another. They ask you to become the kind of reader who refuses both gullibility and scorn. They ask you to build communities that can host rigorous debate without fear, welcome women and men who actually understand what they read, and test every vision by the lives it produces. When a text grows, people who are unbribable, patient, and joyful under pressure keep it close. When a text breeds contempt, addiction to spectacle, or a taste for controlling other consciences, set it aside. That is how hidden words become public blessings.

What remains is simple and demanding. Keep the canon, then widen your shelf. Read the near misses with respect, the desert books with patience, and the official archive with clear eyes. Teach your circle to test voices by the same scales that steady you: Does this word cure ignorance and quiet wrath, does it anchor courage, does it send people into the world ready to reconcile, repair, and endure? If yes, welcome it. If not, let it pass. That was Mary's way of reading, stable and generous. That was Hermas's drill, practical and urgent. That was the Gospel of Truth's tone, joyful and exacting.

Your final image is not a sealed vault or a smoking pile of pages. Picture a table in clear light. On it lie the four Gospels, a copy of Thomas for training attention, Mary for courage under pressure, Truth for the healing of fear, Peter for justice, Hermas for repentance, and a slim notebook with your community's questions and experiments. Around the table sit readers who argue without malice and bless without flattery. That is the voice of the suppressed scriptures when it is finally heard, not a whisper about scandal, but a calm insistence that God is trustworthy, the world can be mended, and knowledge belongs in the service of love.

You wanted the secrets they do not want you to know. Here they are, in plain sight: the canon was a human task inside a faithful community, suppression often looked like budget lines and timid habits, and the most "dangerous" texts are the ones that make ordinary people free. Keep this book visible. Keep the conversation honest. Then let the recovered voices do their work in you, so that your life becomes the most persuasive footnote of all.

FORBIDDEN HISTORY SERIES

Explore other books in the series

Hidden Truths
The Untold Histories, Lost Civilizations, and Forbidden Secrets They Never Wanted You to Discover

Secret Codes
Mystical Manuscripts, Undeciphered Languages, and the Messages That Could Rewrite History

Lost Knowledge
Ancient Technologies, Hidden Sciences, and the Secrets of Civilizations Before Time

Banned Maps
Ancient Charts, Ley Lines, and the Geographic Mysteries That Redefine Our Past

Ancient Echoes
From Göbekli Tepe to the Antikythera Mechanism: The Proof That Advanced Civilizations Existed Long Before Recorded History.

www.ingramcontent.com/pod-product-compliance
Lightning Source LLC
Chambersburg PA
CBHW060752050426
42449CB00008B/1383